WRAPPED IN GOLD

CHARLES T. GILBERT

Charles T. Gilbert

To request permissions, contact the publisher at Staygoldink@proton.me.

ISBN: 979-8-9911512-0-7 (Paperback)

ISBN: 979-8-9911512-1-4 (Ebook)

First paperback edition September 2024

Cover Art by Erika Scipione

Cover Design by Zack Garhart

Manufactured in the United States of America

The names and identifying characteristics of some people described in this book have been changed.

Published by Stay Gold Ink Publishing

Charliegilbert.me

TABLE OF CONTENTS

That Feeling 1

Forty-Seven Years In The Making 2

Say What You Mean 5

Born A Hustler 7

Daydreaming About Death. 10

The Broken Link 14

Unfazed By The Pain 18

That Thing In My Brain 24

This Is Gonna Hurt 27

A Familiar Fear 32

Do You Know Who I Am? 38

New Ways 40

Playing The Part 42

Bobby & The Barber's Shop 49

Hard Lessons 51

The Big Score 56

The End Of The Ride 58

These Are My Consequences 74

The Second Act 80

Empty Promises 85

That Black Cloud 89

Returning To My Element 98

The Chips Are Down 102

From City Slicker To Cowboy 105

Life On The Farm 110

If I Had Known What I Know Now 117

Reaching The Unreachable 123

Looking Inward For Answers 128

The Final Act 134

A Room Full Of Charlies... 137

Confronting Our Flaws... 141

Faith & Gratitude.. 145

The View From The Top.. 147

Acknowledgements & A Taste Of What Is To Come 149

About The Author.. 151

"The only person you are destined to become is the person you decide to be."

— Ralph Waldo Emerson

THAT FEELING

"Strip!" he said. So, I did.

"Now, get in the cell."

"What?" I looked at him like he was crazy. That's not what normally happens. They normally give you a jumpsuit, and some padded foam sandals before sending you into the cage.

But the cop just stood there, looking at me. "Get in the cell, now," he said.

When he locked the door behind me, it hit me: that uncomfortably familiar feeling of being locked up again. Here we go again, I thought. But, at the same time, I started to ask myself: how did I allow it to get *here?* How did I get so desensitized, to *this?*

As soon as the cell door was shut, the cop started being even more of a jerk, asking me how it felt to be a tough guy now that I was in the cell.

I had nothing to say. As I stood in that freezing cage for the next 14 hours, butt naked, all I could do was think about all the ways I wanted to die.

That was the first time I lost everything, but it wouldn't be the last.

FORTY-SEVEN YEARS IN THE MAKING

Being locked up was one thing. Being told by someone I loved that I was nothing but a con man was another. Looking back on it, it was hearing those words, con man, that kicked off this long road of recovery and self-discovery. While the label wasn't deserved, in my eyes, it was how others saw me. And since I knew that's not who I was—a con man—I realized I had to change how I presented myself to others. But to get there, I had to change how I lived. And that's when I started living this life—my best life—a life where I'm able to give back.

This is my story. A story about loss, redemption, forgiveness, and faith.

Forgiveness and faith seem like simple concepts that we can easily apply to the hardships of life. But some of the simplest things in life can be the most difficult—especially for people like me, people who constantly come up with ways to sabotage their best intentions. Once I stopped doing that, a whole new path in life opened up for me. That road was paved with new beginnings, and I had to hit rock bottom more than once to realize what it meant to be truly suffering—and to see what I was truly missing.

But despite the suffering I endured on this journey, this isn't a poor-me story. I had my moments at the top, too—plenty of them. For as many times as I had to start over from nothing, there were times when I was hustling and my pocket was bulging with wads of cash. But all of that came at a price. The price depended on the period in my life, *and* what it took to get what I wanted. At the end of the day, I always found ways to get what I wanted. It was almost always, though, the hard way.

The hard way manifested itself differently throughout my life: sometimes it meant doing time in prison while my family was at home, unwrapping birthday presents around the breakfast table. Other times it meant having to hustle in the streets to pay a bookie on a bad ticket. At one point, it meant losing out on The American Dream—a path that I had constructed with my bare hands—a nice career building multi-million dollar skyscrapers in Manhattan.

In many ways, that specific chapter of my life was the definition of success, especially considering how we are taught and conditioned to view the concept of success. As for how all of *that* went down, we'll get to that chapter later.

But to paint a quick picture of what that chapter of my life looked like, imagine standing in an office overlooking Wall Street on one side, and staring back at the Statue of Liberty on the other side. Having been born and raised in New York, for me this was the pinnacle. The top of the top. In a few short years, the contracting company I had built was earning more jobs than my crew could take on. Times were good during those years, and it was a time when I had everything I ever wanted—on the surface, at least.

Just a few years after the day that cop ordered me to get into the holding cell butt naked, every day I looked over the gleaming New York City skyline. I felt like I could conquer the world—I had finally made it. And I had done it the honest way, too. But for as prosperous as those years were, they didn't produce even half of the success I would see in life. That came at a later time, when I had lost it all, but had finally gained a true understanding of myself, and in effect, my self-worth.

The lows, of course, came, and they came hard.

Still, having been through the mud and back—and dragging other people through it, too—I haven't taken anything for granted. Although there were times when a "sorry" was warranted—and there are plenty—I wouldn't change a single thing about what got me here. What ultimately got me to where I am was years of struggle, addiction, and watching those closest to me walk away or die; but, on the other side of that was the ability to witness firsthand what sort of good can come from giving back. That simple truth took me a while to see, and it didn't truly sink in until someone close to me challenged me to work on myself. As I thought about it, I had always been avoiding that work.

Those words changed my life because I can see now how true they are—I was always looking to do things my way.

SAY WHAT YOU MEAN

My way, though, never seemed to be the right way. While we can all sit here and say we should always do the right thing, treat others how you want to be treated, and take time out of your day to be grateful, it's easy to find ways to avoid doing these things. Because it's not always convenient or comfortable to do the right thing. Anybody can do the right thing when it is on their terms, or when the 'right thing' doesn't require them to be inconvenienced by it. But making time for someone when you're in a hurry or have somewhere to be, can have more of an impact on the world than giving donations to a local church or handing over a dollar to someone who's down on their luck.

Those gestures are noble and valuable, but their impacts are often fleeting. Sometimes those actions miss the mark entirely.

The sort of action I'm talking about is practicing the good—with pure, honest intention—and finding ways to positively impact the people around you on a small scale. The small things can also be the simple things, like paying a compliment to someone on the street or offering to pay for a cup of coffee for the person behind you in line. That type of goodwill, even if it seems like a small ripple in a big pond, has a much greater chance of producing a chain reaction in people. It becomes contagious—when someone sees you do something good, they're more inclined to do the same thing the next time they have the opportunity.

Thankfully, I have that understanding now, but it took me a long time to reach it and to see just what I was doing wrong all those years. Because for so much of my life, I wasn't being good to *me*. It was all about me. The whole game of life was about me, Charlie, and how to win. For more than forty years, I was trying to win by cutting corners in any way that I could. But that whole time, I had been playing the wrong game. Once I figured out my true role in the game, I took the ball and ran with it.

At the same time, it took a while to even figure out what ball I was looking for—that didn't happen until I hit rock bottom, for the umpteenth time. Hopefully, people don't have to go through half the stuff that I had to go through, to find that point of clarity and self-realization that has allowed me to live a full life—a life filled with some of the finer things, but more than anything, filled with family, people I love, and a constant desire to do good. The gifts that I want to bring to this world were *birthed* from that struggle. And despite all the pain, blood, sweat, and tears I shed during those years— decades—of struggling, I wouldn't change a single thing about how my life played out. Not one single thing.

BORN A HUSTLER

If I had to pinpoint when my life started going down the wrong path, I'd say it was when I was thirteen or fourteen years old. Like most kids that age, I wanted nothing more than to fit in. I wanted to find what cool was, and once I did, I wanted to *be cool*. So when I saw the older kids hanging out at the handball court, passing a joint around to the other cool kids, who were surrounded by a couple of pretty girls, I felt like I'd finally found it. I found *cool*. Immediately, I did whatever I could to fall in with that group.

That handball court was nothing special, but we spent a lot of time there. It was set up behind a shop, and there was usually broken glass that we'd have to sweep up if we wanted to play ball. A lot of the time, though, we just hung out there. From the outside, it wasn't much, but it was *ours*. Even though the kids who hung out there were older, I fit in pretty well. I had an older brother, so, naturally, I always found myself wanting to be older than I was. And when I saw those guys with girlfriends, I knew I wanted that. To me, they had it figured out, they made it look easy. I wanted that. So I gravitated towards that group until I became one of them. Being one of them eventually meant getting invited to the keg parties in the woods when I was barely fourteen years old. Beer didn't taste good to me at that age, but drinking was part of being *cool*, so that's what I did.

Little did I know at the time, but even then, I was always avoiding one thing: me. Like most kids, especially young teenagers, I was never truly comfortable with who I was. No matter how "well" things were going on around me, or how much cash I had in my pocket, or which popular, pretty girl I had on my arm that day, I was never truly comfortable with *Charlie.*

In those circles, though, I was comfortable. But I was only comfortable because I could be somebody else, which meant always wearing what *they* were wearing, listening to the music *they* were listening to, and talking or acting like *they* did. I lived like a chameleon, putting on a mask to be someone else, even if it was only for a short time. Once I left those circles and had time to be alone, I could see I wasn't comfortable or happy with myself. Naturally, I did what most people do when they're feeling insecure: I looked for a vice. An escape from the world. Some cheap or quick way to numb the feeling inside of me that something was just *not right.* That was fine, for a while. While it lasted. There were a lot of "good times" that came from living that way. That lifestyle brought me to the clubs, to the coolest parties, and let me be around the "right" people—even though, in many ways, they were not the right people for me. Looking back on it now, it's easy to see that a lot of those people stayed around because of what someone had, not who someone was. Maybe that was a six-pack of beer, or a bag of weed, whatever it was that you could offer them, it made you attractive. And living in that cycle became my reality, for years.

Although I was, for so many years, trying to be somebody else, I at least had an understanding of what drove me, and what made me tick. For as long as I can remember, I've had a passion for anything that you could put on two wheels and ride. As a kid, I'd spend days getting lost in the woods on my bicycle, because that was a place where nobody could find me. To this day, that's my bliss, being on a bike. It doesn't matter if I'm on a dirt bike, bicycle, or chopper, that love for riding has never wavered.

One other part of me that has never changed—although it has taken on different forms—is the hustler mentality. I was born a hustler, and that grind has never stopped. That hustler mentality has put a lot of money in my pockets over the years, even if that money always seemed to find a way to disappear. It was my way to get ahead, even when I was far behind. Even in middle school, I'd be the one slinging bricks of firecrackers to my friends for a little extra cash. As I grew older, the profit on those things got bigger, but so did the risk. For the most part, it was easy money. That's how a hustler lives—easy come, easy go—and it's all I've ever known. That much hasn't changed.

But other things changed. Not long after I smoked that first joint and started hanging out at the handball courts, that casual, easy habit of going out and partying with my friends, smoking dope, and getting drunk, spiraled into something much deeper. And then when my father died, I didn't feel like I had to answer to anyone. So, I didn't.

DAYDREAMING ABOUT DEATH

The day my father died is one that I will never forget. Of course, as is often the case when someone has an experience like this, the small details are etched into my brain. And they will be: forever. But *how* this day played out, exactly, was unusual.

On a typical school day during my sophomore year, I was sitting at my desk, daydreaming. While the teachers were going on with their lessons and giving out homework for the day, I was lost in my own head. That entire day, for whatever reason, I was daydreaming about what it would be like if someone *killed my father*. As strange as it sounds, that's what I was doing in school. Well, for reasons beyond my understanding, that sort of thought was manifesting itself elsewhere.

When I got home from school that day, I got off the bus and saw my uncle's car parked outside my grandmother's house across the street. Now, we all lived close to one another—we were a tight-knit family. Seeing my uncle's car parked outside wasn't out of the ordinary, so I didn't make anything of it. Things started to feel weird, though, when I saw my mom's car parked in our driveway. She worked during the day, and it was still early, which meant she should have still been at work.

I remember walking into the house and seeing my mother, sitting in the dark, alone, on the couch. The room was completely silent. I could tell right away that something was wrong.

When my mother saw me walk in, she flipped on the lamp beside her and said, "Charlie. Sit down. I need to talk to you."

There was no tip-toeing around it. No sugar-coating what had happened. My father had died that morning. He had been working away from home, and when his friends went to check on him in his hotel room, they found him dead. His cause of death: massive heart failure. But I had just seen him just a few days before, and he looked as healthy as ever. So it was shocking, considering he was still relatively young.

The news hit me like a bolt of lightning, but it didn't finally sink in until my mother said to me, "Dad isn't coming home." That was that.

The rest of that week was a mess, dealing with everything leading up to the funeral. I remember family coming in and out of the house at all hours to help with the arrangements for the service. People bringing trays of food and loading up the fridge and freezer. Cards filling up the dining room table. The phone always ringing. Friends and neighbors asking questions. Those next few weeks all just blended together. I missed a lot of school and my grades started to slip. I just wanted to hang out and do things my way.

Losing my father truly changed my life, especially as I was just a sixteen-year-old kid. Beyond just being a huge figure in my life, my father and I were inseparable. We bonded over a lot of things, and we spent countless hours hunting and fishing together. And he wasn't a positive presence for me alone, my father was a huge part of all our lives growing up as kids. From getting us involved in sports to coaching our baseball teams, the man was deeply invested in us, and the community. Beyond just being active in different ways, my father genuinely cared about the community, and he was always trying to make it a better place.

That earnest desire to be a part of the community extended through our family. It became contagious. My mother, my sister, and my brother, we were all fixtures in the community when I was a kid. It was that sort of neighborhood, too, and we took full advantage of immersing ourselves in it, especially when it came to sports and recreational activities. Dad coached our little league baseball team. Mom ran the concession stand. And both my sister and brother hung out at the diamond, even if they weren't playing that day.

Those were formative years. As kids, we grew up on those baseball diamonds. Nearly seven nights a week, that was our home. I can close my eyes now and picture myself as a kid, walking up to bat on those summer nights. That smell of hot dogs and fresh popcorn in the air. That grass was greener than any grass you could find around the city. And when the sun went down and the big lights came on, everything transformed; it might have been Little League, but to me, it felt like the majors.

THE BROKEN LINK

When my father died, that link to the outside world broke. If you weren't the person saying things to me the way I wanted you to say them, then I didn't want to be around you. I began to lose respect for the world, in a lot of ways, after my father died. And so it started, that progression of going out turned into staying out. Sometimes I'd just go to another town—no one really knew where I was, or what I was doing. Every so often I'd visit my brother, who was at college nearby. Otherwise, I'd be with friends from out of town. The like-minded people: the troublesome bunch. But I was usually never where I was supposed to be.

My outlook on life started to change. My grades started to get worse, and I wasn't focused on going to school, getting a good job, and bettering myself like some of my friends were. I was focused on hustling in the streets, and since that meant sometimes having a pocket full of money, I was OK.

As time went on, I distanced myself further from my community. Starting in high school, I began to date girls from other schools, which meant spending even less time at my own school. I hated being there. For as long as I can remember, I didn't really click with a lot of the kids there. Eventually, I was just showing up, smoking weed, and flunking out. Around the start of 12th grade, I decided I'd had enough: I quit school. I was over it, for good. I had other things going on in my life to keep me occupied. I was almost always on the move, not answering to anyone but myself.

That's when the girls really started to play a bigger part in my life. Of course, most teenagers would agree that was a good thing. But it had consequences: before long, I was going from one toxic relationship to another. The first one was as toxic as you could imagine. My girlfriend at that time was a little bit older. I was still just a kid, really, all ego and pride, so I never really treated her right, the way she deserved. At the time, she had her license and drove a car. And even though I didn't have mine, I would drive her car whenever I had the chance.

Now, that's when the cycle really started: I crashed her car, and then I had to pay for the damages. But I never had the money to fix the car. That cycle started to feed itself: make a mistake, and then try to find ways to get the money to pay for that mistake. But, I was never able to actually catch up, it was always rinse and repeat. Being the hustler that I was, it had become second nature to me to make do with what I had. To this day, I still believe that I can 'do' broke better than people can 'do' rich.

Money problems were one thing, building a rap sheet was another. And that cycle began the first time I got busted by the police, which happened not long after my father died. I had just gotten hired to work at a gas station right down the street from my house. It was an easy job with a lot of downtime. Since I'm a quick study, it didn't take long for me to notice that a lot of the cars in the parking lot would be left there with the keys just sitting in them. And it didn't take long for me to come up with the bright idea to take one of them for a joyride. So that's what I did, me and my girl. She hopped in the car with me, and we peeled out of the lot. I felt like a real hot shot, cool as cool could be—until I looked in the rearview mirror, not two seconds later, and saw the flashing blue lights. I was busted before I could even get down the block. Some criminal I was.

But right away, I knew who to call, and it wasn't long before my brother pulled up to the station to come and bail me out. The only reason they didn't throw me in jail was because they couldn't get the owner of the gas station on the phone. The cops actually believed my story, too, that I worked for the gas station and that driving people's cars was just what we did there. The next morning, though, my brother made me go confront the guy whose car it was, and apologize for what I did. I was wrong, but the guy did me wrong and made it worse by saying that I blew up the car. He lied to the cops about how bad it was, so then I had to pay for this and that. It was a whole ordeal, and from there, things just spiraled.

That spiral is what became the ultimate cyclical pattern of always being 'behind the eight-ball'. Being behind the eight-ball meant being in trouble, and then trying to find ways to get out of trouble by making more trouble. That cycle didn't really stop for another twenty years or so. The real trouble was, I got *comfortable* with that cycle. The grind. Always being half broke. They say misery loves company, and I found my misery.

UNFAZED BY THE PAIN

Flash forward a few years, and I was still living the same lifestyle: party, go out, stay out, smoke weed, look for girls, move from job to job, get in a little trouble along the way, and so on. Like most teenagers, me and my buddies thought we were real men, partying like rock stars. There was one particular night that we drank *a lot*. We were loaded before we even got to the bars. Absolutely tanked. We had gotten the bright idea to start drinking Rusty Nails from my friend's dad, who was teasing us about what it meant to be *real men*. Real men, he told us, drink Rusty Nails. None of us knew what a Rusty Nail was, but once he told us, that's all we wanted to drink that night.

Well, one thing led to another, and we soon found ourselves at a club on the other side of town. It was one of *those* nights. Shot after shot. Pounding these things like we were getting paid to do it. Naturally, we met some girls that night. These girls were from out of town, so we wanted to show them a good time by taking them over to our neighborhood. Eventually, we ended up in the car with them. All of us were obliterated—not a single person in that car should have been driving. But we didn't know any better.

That trip was only supposed to be across town, to our neighborhood, just to hang out for a while. But we never made it.

The girl driving the car fell asleep at the wheel. Just like that, the car *flew* across the highway. By the grace of God, we didn't hit anyone else, or anything on the road. But once we made it straight across the highway, the car went all the way through someone's yard and then crashed right into their house. They say we must have been doing between 60-80 mph. How we survived is beyond me.

All the other passengers got lucky, just some bumps and bruises. Not me. The car fully caved in on me. It was so bad that when the ambulance showed up, they had to cut me out of it. Back then, the cops didn't handle a situation like that as they would today. Today, someone would have gone to jail. There would have been serious consequences. But they just rushed us to the hospital—we were just kids, and all that they cared about was us being safe.

I can only imagine how my mother felt when she got that phone call in the middle of the night. "We have your son at Huntington Hospital. You better hurry up. He's pretty banged up."

I was banged up, alright. My jaw had to be wired shut for six weeks, I suffered traumatic brain injuries and needed multiple reconstruction surgeries because of the impact. I suffered all the injuries you would expect from such a serious accident. This might have been my first near-death experience, but for whatever reason, none of it even phased me. The way I saw it, I was just a *passenger* in the car. I wasn't *driving.* It wasn't *my* fault. I spent the following two weeks in hospital. People came to see me, bringing cards, candy, flowers, all that stuff. They loaded me up on painkillers, which I liked. And my poor mother was always there, taking care of me. And even then, seeing the people around me in pain—over my suffering—it still didn't really phase me.

My whole life, I've been able to deal with physical pain. My tolerance is high, for that kind of thing, so it didn't register with me just how bad I was banged up. Neither did it register at the time just how downright selfish I was being. That whole time, I couldn't see what sort of pain this was bringing to the people I loved.

All I thought was: poor me. I'm the one in the hospital bed, with his jaw wired shut, getting brought from one surgery table to the next. The cosmetic scars would heal, and I would be able to chew solid food again, after a while. I would be able to get back on my bike and cruise the block with my friends in no time, so this, to me, was just another bump.

But throughout all of this, I didn't know I was suffering inside. I didn't know I wasn't *happy.* That whole time, I was still trying to find *my way* of doing things. A way to cut corners, some sort of shortcut to the whole game. A secret code to finding happiness. Whatever it was, *I* was going to figure it out. I didn't need anyone to tell me the right way to do things because I was going to find it on my own. In my eyes, all those people working normal jobs, punching clocks, putting in their time for someone else, they were suckers.

And I was programmed to think that way—programmed to think that I was going to hit it big and live happily ever after. That meant constantly looking for the next big score. The next scam. The next scheme. Hustling, all the time. Whatever I could get my hands on, I could turn into a hustle. I had a knack for it, too.

It fueled me to find that score because I was being told by society that I was never going to amount to anything, and that I was a loser. But little did they know, I was going to win in the end. And I sold myself that story. So I was trying to take what I could get, all the time. At that point, all I truly worried about was going to prison. *That* scared me.

In the same way that I could deal with pain, I had a natural ability to ride the ups and downs that came with going broke after being flush for a while. I was largely unfazed by the financial struggles that came and went because I always found ways to get through it—one way or another.

For so much of my life, and especially then, my mindset was: I'll show you guys. I'll get my score. I was always looking for the next quick come-up or another way to fill my pockets to make me feel like I was on top for a little while. Well, that pattern became established. It became so ingrained in me and my way of living that I didn't stop to see what it was doing to the people around me.

As long as I can remember, my brother has been in my ear, trying to lead me in the right direction. Not long after my father died, my brother quit school. That decision is what led him to become a police officer. My brother has always been smart, so he crushed it at the academy—it was a quick rise for him, and it came naturally. His little brother, meanwhile, was still running the streets, rolling with the same trouble that he found on those handball courts as a young teenager. Not only was my brother setting an example of how to be through his actions—pay your bills on time, build a family, and be good to the community—but that whole time, he was the one trying to set me straight.

My mother also constantly tried to talk some sense into me. We clashed, of course. She busted my balls a lot. But that was out of love. People around me would say that she loved me the most. Whether *that* was true or not, I realize now that I cared for her, at that time, more than anyone else in my life. That's likely because my brother had his family, and my sister had her own life.

No matter how many times I screwed up, my mother never stopped trying to keep me straight—even if that meant giving me a little tough love. But I wasn't listening. I was determined to figure it out *my way,* avoiding accountability, and always looking for that shortcut. So from age eighteen to twenty-two, Monday through Sunday, it became all about finding an escape. *Where's the next party—where's the next bag of dope—where's the next place to get our drink on?*

I took on plenty of random jobs during those years, mostly in construction. It turned out that I excelled in that field—I was good with my hands and very detail-oriented. I'm a perfectionist. Those skills would come in handy later, but none of those jobs really stuck. Because it always came down to finding the easy way out. The fast money. The hot girls. The next thrill. Because I wasn't going to live like the rest of the suckers, punching a time clock every day. I was going to do things *my way*.

THAT THING IN MY BRAIN

This stretch of my life was formative in many ways. I was piling bad choices onto a poor lifestyle, and refusing to confront the truths in my life. The evidence was there, I just didn't want to face it. Then something happened that changed everything. In the wake of the car accident, when they wired my jaw shut and did multiple reconstructive surgeries on my face, I had a grand mal seizure in the recovery room. That's when the doctors found something abnormal in my brain. The medical term for what they found was a cavernous angioma—although, at the time, the doctors didn't know much about it other than it was a benign tumor.

This is something that is still in me, to this day, and it won't ever go away. It sits in the front lobe of my brain. From the surgeries, the doctors figured it had gotten irritated, causing it to bleed. At the time, even though they knew little about it or how serious it could be, I wasn't exactly freaked out. This was just another bump. A physical ailment I could get through, with enough time to heal. I only wanted to get through my recovery so I could get back to how I'd been living my life before the accident.

About eight months after they found the cavernous angioma, I was lying in bed with my girl at home. We fell asleep, and it was in my sleep that I had a seizure. Of course, my girl started freaking out. My mother was home at the time, and she rushed me to the hospital right away. We saw the same doctor who had treated me for the first seizure. Since that first seizure, I had been following up with neurologists, but the seriousness of what could be going on with me never really sunk in, even if the doctors and my mother were going into panic mode.

They wanted to cut me open right away and take this thing out. My mother and I both knew what this meant: if they went ahead with the procedure, it could kill me. So, when the doctors insisted on it, without hesitating, both my mother and I said, "No way. Not a chance."

Even if we *were* going to go that route, it wasn't going to be in that hospital. If anyone was going to cut my skull open and do such a dangerous procedure, it was going to be the best doctors in the world. That was nothing against *my* doctor—he saved my life—but if we were going to make a big decision like that, the procedure would have to be done by the very best. Period.

So, I took the medications they prescribed, even though some of them had pretty gnarly side effects and made me feel horrible. In fact, some of those meds they gave me are banned now. You can imagine what sort of things they did to my body—not only did they make me *feel* horrible, they *were* horrible. But I did what I was told, and I took them, and went to all of my follow-ups.

I thought, as long as I do what I'm supposed to, I won't get sick. No need to worry about having another seizure, so long as I listened to what the doctors said. So to me, that meant I could live my life like I had been: going out to the clubs, partying all night, living like a crazy person. Even when it came to doing things like going to visit my brother at college, or going mountain biking and snowboarding, I kept partying. I didn't see much reason in getting caught up with something I didn't understand, especially something so random. I just kept living my life, not thinking about the consequences of my actions or what I might be doing to my body in the process.

Soon after, the doctors had figured out more about this cavernous angioma. By then, they understood that you did *not* want to remove it. If it was inside of you, you just lived with it. And the best way to live with it was to keep an eye on it and stick to the medications. That meant tons of MRI scans and doctor visits to make sure it wasn't growing.

Another year or so went by, and I got sick again, in my sleep. Every time I got sick, it meant days in the hospital, hooked up to the machines, and going through all sorts of tests and scans. After a while, it was starting to weigh on me—the whole thing was taxing, both physically and mentally. I felt uneasy that they kept upping my meds, but since the internet wasn't what it is today, I didn't have the means to do more research. I had to just stick to what they said, and do my part. But in the back of my mind, the thought was creeping up on me: is this really *bad? Is this thing going to be what kills me?*

THIS IS GONNA HURT

While my friends were out, getting good jobs, working towards buying their first cars, and being *normal* members of society, I was out doing my thing. Still hustling in the streets, keeping some cash in my pocket, and feeling like a big shot. It didn't always come easy, but it was always enough to keep me happy—on the surface.

One night, when I was eighteen or nineteen years old, a lot of underlying issues came to a head—the loss of my dad, the people who'd treated me wrong or bullied me growing up, the fact that nothing came easy for me, watching my friends get the stuff they wanted, the fights with my girl. I was dating an older girl at the time, someone I met through my brother while he was in college, but the relationship was toxic. That night, we happened to be arguing in the front yard.

She was in her car, and we were fighting about something stupid. It was always *something stupid.* Out of the corner of my eye, I saw these three kids strolling down the street, clearly looking for trouble. The streetlights were on, but there were no cars out on the road. People were asleep and the rest of the block was quiet, when all of a sudden, one of the kids smashed a forty-ounce bottle of beer in the street. The sound boomed down the block. And that's when I lost it. Everything washed over me all at once, like a tidal wave.

My fists were clenched as I walked up to them. I was gonna teach them a lesson. I yelled something at them and it kicked off. Before I knew it, the three of them were surrounding me. By then, my girl was upset. She had gotten out of the car and was trying to hold me back. But I wasn't going to let up, I was like a mad dog that had broken its leash. It turned into a big ordeal pretty quickly, and before long, a few of the neighbors who had been asleep were outside to see what all the noise was about. A couple of punches were thrown before I got one of the kids on the ground. But the next thing I knew, one of the other kids pulled out a knife. Just like that, the blade went into the side of my stomach. Being the tough guy I was, I decided to provoke him even more.

Staring the kid down, I said to him, "What, you need a knife? Go ahead, stab me again. See what happens."

Well, I saw what happened. The blade went right into my stomach. The kid stabbed me again. But that didn't stop me. My adrenaline was raging. I was still acting like a wild animal, totally out of my mind, trying to fight them off.

By the time the ambulance showed up, the kids were gone— they'd made off down the block. My mother had made it to the front yard and was asking my girl what had happened. She was freaking out, seeing me on the ground like that in a pool of blood. When the cops rolled up, they started interrogating me. I was still out of my mind, acting like a punk to them.

Bleeding out, there I was, giving the cops shit about how they should be out looking for those kids instead of busting my chops. But they *knew me*. They knew Charlie Gilbert, and they knew I was half a punk. Even though I was giving them a hard time, the officers were cool to me—they just wanted me to calm down. By then, blood was filling my lungs. My liver and spleen had both been penetrated by the knife. Even though I was having a hard time breathing, I was still keeping it together. I was coherent, but all I could concentrate on was arguing with the police and being a jackass.

Finally, they put me on the gurney and got me in the ambulance. Blood was pouring out of my sides. I was slowly dying. I looked around the ambulance and recognized familiar faces. Alice Lanning and Derrick Thorton were both kids from the block. While I was running in the streets, causing trouble and chasing the next score, they had both become paramedics—and here they were, keeping me alive.

My mother was waiting for us when we arrived at the emergency room. They got me on the bed and stuck the IV in me. All the while, I was coherent, but I was having a hard time breathing. And that whole time, I felt a sharp pain in my spine—it felt like an ice pick had been jammed in my back. The doctors and my mother were all telling me to calm down, to quit acting crazy, because I kept crying about how much my back hurt.

They all kept saying, "But, Charlie, you were stabbed in the stomach. What do you mean, your back hurts?"

That's when the surgeon burst into the room. It was like something you'd see on TV. He started calling out orders: give me this, hold that, move this, get back, do that. He didn't waste any time in getting people in their places.

Once he realized who my mother was, the surgeon turned and said to her, very seriously, "We have to insert a chest tube. *Right now*. He will not make it if we don't."

I remember my mother walked up to me and said, "Charl, you always ask me to be straight with you, so I'm going to tell you: THIS IS GONNA HURT."

And I was like, *"What?"*

Right as I said that, the security staff and nurses all bum-rushed me. The next thing I knew, there were hands all over me, holding me down on the bed. I kept fighting, but they had me pinned down like a rag doll.

The surgeon walked right up to me and said, "Charles. Your mother is right. This is going to hurt. But I *promise* you, it'll be over before you know it."

Then I saw him pull out a scalpel. In his other hand, there was a long, plastic tube. I remember it being hard, like a plastic hanger. But I was losing so much blood that they didn't have any time to waste. They didn't even have the time to numb me—I had no anesthesia, nothing. The doc just went straight in with the knife. He cut me open like a fish—from the top of my chest down to the belly button—and then shoved this tube in me. That tube was hooked up to a pump. And sure enough, the surgeon was right.

I felt *instant relief.* I felt the warm blood running down my side. That whole process felt like it took forever, but it really only lasted about ten seconds.

I immediately calmed down after that. All that pain in my back had disappeared, instantly. Everything felt better. About half the blood in my body had been sucked out by that tube. By then, I knew it was serious, and that if they hadn't inserted the tube, I wouldn't have made it. And I knew that because, while all this was happening, they had brought the priest into the hospital room, and he had his hands on me. Even my mother was in my ear, saying goodbye. Just in case.

A FAMILIAR FEAR

A few years later, when I was out mountain biking with some friends, I wiped out pretty badly. I hit a tree, and it knocked me out cold. Once I came to, I got back up and kept riding—I didn't think anything of it. No big deal, just a few bumps and bruises. Then, two days later, I was at my home—and much of this, I don't remember. Certain details I would only learn when I was lying in a hospital bed a few days later. But it was at home after the mountain biking spill that I had another seizure—this was one of two times that I got sick when I was awake. I had been standing at the top of the stairs—which was a basement-type apartment with concrete floors—and I had a seizure. I went tumbling straight to the bottom and then smacked my head on the floor.

Thankfully, my friend Freddy had come over to visit me. He had the day off and had decided to swing over and see what I was getting up to that night. When he got there, he found me at the bottom of the stairs, bleeding. Since I was still living a pretty loose life at the time, Freddy feared the worst: someone had robbed me and knocked me unconscious.

I woke up at the hospital, surrounded by doctors and my mother. There were stitches all down my face. I got busted up pretty badly when I fell, and I was wearing a neck brace. Still to this day, no one knows *exactly* what happened. I was totally confused, with no recollection of what happened between being at the top of the stairs and then waking up in the hospital. It was a little scary, and my mother calmed me down once I fully came to—all she could tell me was that Freddy had come by at just the right time.

"Was I being an asshole?" I asked her, since I tended to be an asshole when I was in the hospital for my seizures. Even the doctors and nurses knew me as being that way—ornery when it came to small stuff, like needing a blanket.

"No," she said. "You were calm." But then she told me that the doctors were pushing to operate on me and take this thing out. I was beginning to get nervous. This time it hit a little differently, and that thought was steadily creeping in, "*What* is going on?"

It was hard *not* to feel drained from the constant cycle of getting sick and then being better, only to get sick again. And almost always, it was random. After we left the hospital and I got my stitches out, my mother sat me down, and we had a serious conversation.

She said, "Charlie. Would you feel better if we went with another doctor?" Again, we loved my primary neurologist at the time. It wasn't anything *he* was doing, it was just the feeling that we could be doing something better.

"Ma, I think that's what we need to do," I said. And so that's what we did.

My mother did her homework, and not long after, we flew to Colombia, where they had the best doctor in the world for this kind of thing. The hospital there had a whole brain unit on the ninth floor, and most of the people in there were just like me. Some of them were just *kids*. And while I only had *one* of these things, some of the kids in that unit had up to twenty-three of them in their brains. They were truly dying. It was hard to see, but as nervous and unsettled as I was, my doctor assured me that I should be grateful—it could have been much worse.

My doctor was also able to explain more about the cavernous angioma. He told me that they had no idea when this one started to form in my brain, but they would also never know, so there was no use in trying to figure it out. My doc was able to calm me down and help me gain a better perspective on the whole situation.

But I still wanted answers. I wanted the truth. Since I'd had so much experience with doctors by this point, I decided to have a one-on-one talk with him, without anyone else in the room. One day, after everyone had left, I gave it to him straight.

I said, "Doc. Be honest with me. If I were your son, what would *you* do? Would you cut this thing out?"

He didn't even hesitate. "Absolutely not. I would stick to your medications," he said. "Don't mess that up. I know they suck, Charlie, but *stick to your meds.*"

Even though I listened to him, and my other doctors, and did the right thing by sticking to my meds, I was still suffering. I was still getting sick, even while I was taking the meds. Naturally, one thought kept gnawing away at me: *I'm messed up. Am I going to be like this forever?*

The whole cycle was starting to take a toll on me. I was afraid to go to sleep. The thought of even taking a nap freaked me out—because I thought if I did, I might never wake up.

Back home in New York, I decided to have a serious conversation with the doctors again. I was young and sometimes an asshole, but they respected that about me, that I could ask them to give it to me straight. At the time, my primary doctor could tell that something was going on with me. I was being a little more difficult than usual, and he could tell that I was off.

"Charl, what's going on?" he asked me, once the room was empty and the two of us were alone. "The nurses are complaining. You're being kind of an asshole."

I said, "OK. Do you want me to be honest with you?"

"Of course, I do."

"Doc, I'm afraid to go to sleep. I don't want to get sick," I said. "I keep thinking that any time I want to take a nap, I need to say my goodbyes, just in case."

My doctor laughed and the tension immediately lightened. "Dude, I can't read your mind. You have to tell me when stuff like this is going on. I can help you with that. I'll give you something to help that go away."

I hadn't even *considered* that. This whole time, I had just been dealing with it, like I did everything else. All I thought to do was tough it out—that was my way of dealing with pain, or anything difficult: by facing it head-on.

Then he said, "Charlie, I'm going to fix this right now, and I'll sit with you until you feel better." A minute later, my doctor put something in my IV.

"Do you feel better now?" he asked.

"Oh, yeah..."

Then, darkness.

I woke up to my family and a bunch of people looking down on me, and I was lying in the hospital bed.

"What *time is it?*" I asked.

My mom laughed. It was the *next day*. But I'd needed it. I was so sleep-deprived that my body was in desperate need of that kind of rest. The anxiety and nerves I had for my situation were finally starting to slow down.

It also helped that my doctor later told me, "Look, Charlie, you're not going to die anytime soon. Do you have something that could take you out at any time? Yes. Do I think it's going to? No. You're going to live a good life. You need to stay on top of this, and stick to your meds."

For as much as I wanted to do the right thing and stick to what the doctors were saying, it was hard sometimes to live with the side effects. I would often feel downright awful, so it wasn't long after my doctor gave me strict orders to keep on the meds that I stopped taking them. No one knew about this, except for me. But the way I saw it, I was getting sick no matter what—with or without the meds. I accepted that I was going to get sick—sometimes twice a year, but it mostly happened once a year. At the time, I failed to see that I was carrying around this weight with me: the stress, the feelings of unhappiness, the toxic lifestyle I was living—all of this only perpetuated the cycle.

DO YOU KNOW WHO I AM?

Gradually, I started to make changes and began to shed toxic presences from my life like they were dead weight, and things were starting to change in my life because of those decisions. I was getting on the straight and narrow, which meant no drinking and no drugs. The better I treated myself, and my body, the better I began to feel about myself and how I interacted with the world. I was starting to feel like I had something to give back after all the shit I had gone through.

Jumping forward a few years to when I was in my twenties, I was with my buddy, speaking to men transitioning from prison. By this point, I had a good routine. My life was getting put back together, and I was happy with where it was going. And importantly, I was now *on the other side*, speaking to guys behind bars. There were maybe 100 guys in the group we were speaking to that day, and when we were wrapping up for the day, one of the guys from the prison came up to me.

He looked at me and said, "Do you know who I am?"

I looked him up and down, racking my brain to think where I might have recognized him from. Nothing registered. I had no idea who he could be—he looked like just another guy in prison orange to me.

"No, I don't know who you are," I said.

"I'm *the guy*." It took me a minute to realize what he said. But then it hit me: staring back at me was the kid who sent me to the hospital after I had dared him to stab me with a knife. Back when I thought I had something to prove to the world.

I sort of smirked when I said to him, "Well, you ain't changed much." The thing is, I wasn't even mad—I wasn't angry at the guy or anything that happened that night. Because the way I saw it, at that moment, this person was just as lost and scared as I was. He was just like me. A punk kid, out there in the world, trying to take more than he was giving.

Part of me also knew that he *could be* just like me—the me I was at that moment in my life—doing what I was doing, giving back, at least in the ways that I could at the time.

My disease, as I was starting to see it, was that I was trying to take on everything—by myself, like a real man. I was unable to ask for help. Asking for help meant showing vulnerability, and that wasn't even something that crossed my mind. But this wasn't how I wanted to live anymore. Because it was an epic failure, every time *Every fucking time.*

NEW WAYS

Around that time, I was starting to figure out a better formula for how to live and how to be an honest, contributing member of society. That's when I met my future wife. Despite all the changes throughout my life, having a girl by my side was one of the few things I depended on for happiness and stability. My way of being comfortable was having my girl on my arm, and as long as we were getting along, that was my security blanket. But when it was taken away from me, I would lose control. Everything would be blown to pieces. I was like a scared little puppy, and I would do whatever it took to get her back.

A few girls came and went before I met my first wife, but those relationships were all toxic. Toxic as in slashing tires, smashing windows, calling the police on one another, getting into screaming matches—you name it. That was my life, on repeat, with a few different girls, until I found that one. The good girl who made me straighten out a bit. For a while, at least.

She wasn't like the others. She had her head on straight, and so I started to chill out too. I began to see that it wasn't all about *me*. Things progressed pretty quickly, and she and I settled down not long after getting together. But we were just kids. She got pregnant, and then pregnant again. We got married after that. But it was just another story of kids having kids, and we weren't prepared. We got by the best we could, and it was a struggle, but that new life brought about the facade of having my stuff together.

The house, the wife, the two kids. I worked different hustles, sometimes legitimate, sometimes not. That inconsistency meant we sometimes didn't even have diaper money. There were days when I would have to park the car two blocks around the corner to hide it from the repo guys when they came knocking. Supporting two small babies, and being so young, was not easy. We didn't have much, but she and I made it work.

And yet, as hard as things were, for the first time in my life, I felt like I was sort of doing things right. I was being the best father I could be, and the best husband I could be. I was gradually beginning to be able to provide more for my family, financially. But that meant falling back in with some of the same routines, surrounding myself with the same people that I had seen run the block as a teenager. The sort of people that I should *not* have been around. But the lifestyle that I had established, the one that came with fast money and late nights, was too good to give up. That hustle in me never died, it just took a different form.

PLAYING THE PART

A lot has been made of New York in the 80s and 90s, with organized crime and drugs running rampant. Hollywood has turned out a hundred movies about mobsters and some of the famous syndicates of that time. But make no mistake about it, there is truth in a lot of them. "Tough guys" were real, and there were codes to stick by.

Whether they were articulated or not, certain lines were drawn, and it didn't take much to figure out what would happen if they were crossed. Thankfully, I never truly crossed those lines—although, a few times, I came pretty close.

Since that sort of life had always attracted me, I found ways to be around it, especially as a teenager. That meant gambling more than I could afford and then living like a hotshot hustler when it came to finding ways to cover my losses. The more time I spent around that glamorized way of living, the more drawn into it I became: the fast money and that ever-elusive idea of the *big score*. The way I saw it, I could hit that $100,000 jackpot on a parlay, and then live the good life. But that never happened, which usually left me behind the eight-ball more often than not.

At the same time, I knew what it meant *not* to pay. So when it came time to pay, I did what I had to do. There was one time I was roughly twenty-thousand dollars down—I was barely 18 years old. That Wednesday, I went to see the guys in charge of collecting, and that's when it started to sort of click for me. As happy as they were to see me, the bookies didn't care about *me*, or how much I lost or won. *They just wanted their money*. I was able to see that because when I went to pay up that day, they were surprised that I had it all—all twenty grand. Imagine, a teenager, walking around New York City with that kind of cash in his pocket. People didn't often pay on time, which is probably what surprised the bookies. But I knew damn well: the one thing you didn't want to do was piss those guys off. Because they would come and collect, one way or another. And I knew that Wednesday was the day they came to collect. So that's exactly what I did: I paid up, in full.

Looking back on it now, especially being where I am, it's not a stretch to think that I could have been a millionaire a hundred times over had I actually been smart with the money I was making. Had I put away a few of those scores instead of putting it all on black, maybe it could have become something more than just a quick score that would get squandered in no time. But to me, it was always about the fast money and feeling like a *real man*, which meant living in the face of danger, even if I didn't always see it that way.

Underground poker clubs were becoming all the rage at that time, especially in New York, since gambling was illegal. That only meant that the gray area became bigger and easier to tap into, especially if you knew the right people. Because of the rising popularity of games like Texas Hold 'Em, there were always people who wanted a piece of the action. And we knew how to give it to

43

them. But, to keep an operation running smoothly—without catching any heat from the cops or the wrong people—meant keeping things legit. Or, as legit as they could be. This meant no sports gambling, no electronic machines, and certainly no alcohol or drugs. Absolutely no other illegal activity—that was rule number one for running an underground club in New York at the time. We all knew that.

Because if the place *did* get infiltrated by the police, and they busted in, all they'd find was ten guys sitting around, smoking cigars, playing cards, and talking about their wives. As long as we weren't breaking the pot or doing anything wrong, they wouldn't find anything too incriminating. Now, if they had a rat or someone on the inside, that was a different story. But we kept tight circles—I knew everyone coming in and out of my clubs.

A lot of those familiar faces were guys I grew up around. Mostly friends and friends of friends, but then there were people like Tommy D., one of the older cats from the block. Now, Tommy D. was someone that I always looked up to—until I didn't. Even though I had my own thing and ran everything on my own, Tommy D. was one of the guys who watched over everything. He had some sway back then, and quite a few people answered to Tommy D.

Tommy D. was adamant about not having any drugs in the clubs, that was his biggest thing. For the most part, I kept good on that. When I didn't, I would be discreet about it. But it was never anything crazy when it came to that kind of stuff, just the occasional joint, pill, or drink that I would sneak in while I was working the floor. Even when it was with a friend, we always kept it on the down-low because we knew what would happen if we didn't.

At the time, I had a friend named Richard, who was with me at the club one night when I was working the floor. Richard and I popped into the bathroom to sneak a few bumps. It was a slow night, so we were hanging out for a minute in there, just bullshitting while we busted up a couple of lines. I took mine, and then he took his. But Richard wasn't done. I knew that I had to get back out on the floor since I was working, so I left him in there. As soon as I stepped out of the bathroom, the first person I saw was Tommy D.—with a few of his guys.

Now, this was normal. Tommy D. and his guys would swing through the club and check up on us to make sure everything was running straight. We put out a giant spread of food for the guys at the same time every night, so Tommy D. and his crew were there as usual, grabbing something to eat, and doing their check-up.

But things were about to go south, real quick. Because Tommy D. and his guys walked straight into the bathroom. As soon as I saw them go in there, my stomach dropped. I *knew* what they were going to find in there. But all I could think about was me. Going through my head was, "Fuck. This is it. They're going to shut me down. My club days are over, no more money for me. It was a good run while it lasted."

Of course, they found Richard in the bathroom with his nose buried in a line of cocaine. It took all of two seconds for Tommy D. and his guys to burst out of the bathroom and yank me by the collar. They dragged me in there to show me just what they had found. By that time, they had already laid a few punches on Richard. They were pissed off, and now they were looking to prove a point.

The thing is, Richard would have been done with two punches, but they didn't stop there. Those guys let him have it. They beat down on Richard while looking at me, saying, "Yo! You're going to let this shit fly? You realize what'll happen if it does? You'll be in fucking *jail*. You gotta handle this!"

Handling it meant I had to step in and kick Richard a few times. I felt horrible about it, truly horrible, but I had no choice. Richard and I had known each other for a long time, and I knew that if I were ever in trouble, he was someone I could call. He would come to help, no questions asked. Had Richard told him that he *knew* me and that I had just been in the bathroom with him with a line up my nose, I would have been right there on the ground with him, with my head next to the toilet and blood pouring out of my face. Because it didn't matter who I was—I had been told once, and once was enough. You didn't cross lines. Not with these guys.

My heart was in my throat watching Richard get the snot beat out of him, begging them to stop. I was nervous because I knew just how easy it would have been for Richard to say my name or do something to give me up. Even a simple glance could have been

46

enough to tip these guys off. But thankfully, Richard acted like he didn't know who I was.

Even after laying into him for a while, Tommy D. and his guys didn't quit. They dragged him out of the restroom and into the club, in front of everyone, to show them what would happen if you *did* cross those lines. Because the guys who came to the club to play poker didn't want that. They weren't there for the drugs, or for the horse races on TV, or the under-the-table stuff, none of that nonsense. The guys there just wanted a clean club where they could play cards, nothing else. So, to keep things running smoothly, sometimes that meant making an example out of someone. It didn't take long for Tommy D. and his guys to get their point across. They busted Richard up pretty badly; he was in rough shape by the time they quit.

And all I could do was play the part. Acting like I didn't know him, while I put in a few kicks on my friend, saying things like, "Yeah, punk! You better learn your lesson not to bring that shit around here." Thinking about it now, it makes me sick. I still dream about it, being in that bathroom, wanting to do something to help Richard, but knowing that I flat out could not. For weeks, I felt horrible about the whole thing.

Richard stopped coming around the club. After that, things between us were never the same, even though he insisted that there were no hard feelings. Richard understood. He had been around these guys long enough and he knew what it meant to mess around under their noses.

When it came up, Richard would say, "No, it's all good. It was my fault, man. We shouldn't have been messing around. I shouldn't have been influencing you like that. It's fine."

When really, that could have been *me* influencing *him*. Just because he was the one who got caught with that stuff up his nose didn't mean that I couldn't have been in his shoes had things played out a little bit differently. And that was the truth. I *knew* these people, and I knew where their heads were at when it came to this stuff. It was serious business. And that's what it was supposed to be: *business.*

BOBBY & THE BARBER'S SHOP

Business was booming for a while during those years. I even opened up a few clubs of my own. One of those clubs was in the back of a barber's shop, which was tucked into a strip of laundromats, bowling alleys, barber's shops, bodegas, and nail salons. The sort of strip you'd find in most boroughs of New York City.

One night, we were there doing our thing, and a car rolled up out front. Inside the car was one of the real tough guys in New York at the time. It was well understood that this was not someone you crossed.

He and his guys got out of the car and walked into the club, and right away they asked where Georgie, one of the guys from the block, was. When they found him, they said, "Georgie, come outside. We gotta talk to you."

We didn't need to know the details, we knew it was bad. Because back in the day, there were the wanna-be tough guys, and then there were the real ones. The ones who made things happen— the ones that you didn't want to cross or piss off.

Georgie knew this. And he knew he was in trouble. But he kept his cool, he didn't freak out or try to get away. Georgie was outside there with them for maybe twenty minutes. When he came back inside, he was all busted up. He kept his composure, but he was in rough shape. I mean, real rough shape. His jaw was practically hanging off the side of his face—they let him have it pretty bad.

"Yo, Georgie, you gotta go to the hospital," we said. "What the hell happened?"

"Oh, it was nothing," he said. "I owed those guys like fifteen grand."

Fifteen grand? I thought back to the days of owing twenty grand, and I couldn't get it out of my head that it could have so easily been me sitting there with my jaw hanging off. And there was Georgie, keeping it together, living with the consequences of his actions. Later, we came to find out that he had owed those guys for about three weeks. *That* was why you paid up *that week*. You didn't play games with those guys, or you'd find out the hard way.

Watching Georgie walk around with his jaw wired shut for the next eight weeks still didn't really phase me. Of course, I felt bad for Georgie, but I was more impressed that one of these tough guys was at my club. I felt like a hot shot, having someone like him roll up and play cards at *my club*.

HARD LESSONS

Even if I wasn't always the one brushing up against danger, it usually found its way to me, one way or another. And I watched my friends, like Georgie, get into trouble by messing around a little too much, which meant some of them had to learn the hard way too.

Bobby was one of those friends. Growing up, we hung out a lot and ran in some of the same circles. But Bobby wasn't exactly being smart about things around the time we started to become adults. He wasn't being as careful about certain things as he should have been; at least, not as careful as the people above him *wanted* him to be.

Now, at that time, the whole block was essentially run by the same people, which meant they had a pretty close eye on things. Anything that happened on that block, big or small, they knew about. For a while, Bobby was having girls come through the house, late at night. This was a big no-no because it pretty much meant one thing, that these were the type of girls who you did *not* want hanging around.

Besides, it would only take one slip-up with the wrong person to put someone else's thing in jeopardy. The guys up top didn't want some random girl off the street to get *them* caught up in something that wasn't even their business. So when they found out that Bobby was messing around, bringing these girls by the house at all hours of the night, they had something to say about it.

That day, my buddy Freddy and I were hanging out at the house playing cards. One of the older guys, Vince, was there too. It was the kind of place where people would pop in and out and spend a few hours playing cards or shooting the shit.

In the middle of our game, Tommy D. walked in. "Where's Bobby?" he asked.

We looked at each other and knew right away that it wasn't good. "I don't know," I said. "Upstairs?"

"Go get him." So I did what he said, and ran upstairs right away to get Bobby.

When Bobby came downstairs, he said, "What's up, Tommy?"

"Listen, you can't be stupid around here," said Tommy D. "You got it?"

Bobby must have given him a look because Tommy D. snapped back, "Don't look at me stupid. I *know* what you're up to." Then Tommy D. turned to Vince. "You gotta talk some sense into your people, Vince." He turned back to Bobby. "I've seen the cars. Those hookers you got rolling through here at all hours of the night? That shit ends. Right *now*."

Bobby didn't argue. "OK, OK," he said. "I understand."

About a month later, I was back at the house, hanging out with Freddy and a few of the guys. We saw Tommy D. come in the door and knew right away what it meant when he asked where Bobby was.

Tommy D. didn't even have to ask me what to do. I ran upstairs and got Bobby. As soon as Bobby came down, Tommy D., gritting his teeth, asked him, "What did I tell you?"

Right away, Bobby knew it was bad. So did I. Because when I looked over to Tommy D., I saw him holding a piece of plywood with a piece of wire wrapped around one side of it. BAM. He hit Bobby right in the face with it. BAM, he let him have it again. Then Tommy D. pushed Bobby backward, right into the bathroom. But he didn't stop, he kept beating him with it. Blood was squirting out of Bobby's face, spraying against the walls, leaking all over the floor. Of course, Bobby was crying, begging him to stop, saying he was sorry.

But Tommy D. kept going at it. Then he stopped and told Bobby to get in the bathtub. Standing over him in the tub, Tommy D. looked down at Bobby and said, "Now you know I'm serious."

And then, just like that, Tommy D. walked out of the house.

We ran to help Bobby up onto his feet. Freddy gave him something for his face. All I could ask him was, "Did you seriously keep doing that shit? What are you, stupid? They have this whole block on watch. There's no lying to these guys, Bobby. You're going to get them connected to some small, petty thing and get someone locked up. You cannot be messing around like that."

53

And that was the end of that. Bobby didn't bring any girls around the house anymore. He recovered, and Tommy D. treated him the same as he did before—they both acted like nothing ever happened. That was part of being in that life. You dealt with the consequences if you messed up. So, you tried not to mess up. I thank God that I never crossed anybody, even though there were times I thought I was going to. Because just when you thought you were the big guy, the bigger guy showed up.

That was how it went, for years—being in the streets, hustling, being around people who had my back but also *did not* have my back. I had my run at it. But I never ended up being where I wanted to be, and I certainly never hit that big score when it came to gambling or hustling. I was always jammed up.

Eventually, I slowed down when it came to that kind of stuff. I quit running the clubs, but I didn't totally get out of the game. There were still ways to hustle without being the one staring down danger all the time. It also helped that, around that time, I had a buddy who opened up his own club on Long Island. This place was big—like, fifteen rooms type of big, which is bigger than some of these casinos you see today.

Since I wasn't running my own thing, I went to work for him for a while, dealing cards. I did well there. Real well. But being at the clubs all night—from six p.m. to six a.m.—meant that I would come home at the crack of dawn, and I'd be missing out on being with my family. On top of that, the more I was making, the more I was spending. Since things were coming in fast, I was spending it just as fast. I wasn't saving the money like a lot of my friends were at the time. It was just that same chaotic cycle, and I was finding comfort in that, even if I didn't fully realize the magnitude of what I was doing.

As good as things were, on paper, I still wasn't *happy* or *comfortable* with myself—there was still so much going wrong inside. The drinking, the drugs, and the gambling all found their way back into the picture, picking it right back up where they left off. And I found ways to justify it, ways to make it feel *normal*. But it wasn't normal. I'd be out, making wads of cash while my wife was back home, feeding the kids. Bathing them. Doing the things that a mother should be doing. Naturally, that resentment built up. And then you add in the financial swings and the struggles that came from that lifestyle, and it just never seemed like we could catch up. There was always *something*.

THE BIG SCORE

That something became something much bigger when I got into buying and then selling fireworks on the black market. It was a risky hustle, but one that I was good at; just like dealing cards and running underground clubs, I used it as another way to provide for my family. I wasn't doing it for me. Sure, I enjoyed some of the luxury things I could buy with the money we made, but this was about giving my family the things that they deserved. Giving them a taste of the *good life*, since we had spent so many years struggling, sometimes without two nickels to rub together.

Around that time, the gambling slowed down for me. I was slowly phasing it out because people were looking for safer ways to gamble on poker and a few of those underground clubs shut down. They'd go over to Atlantic City, Foxwoods, or one of the cities nearby where you could do it at a legit casino. On top of that, the cops were starting to catch onto what we were doing, and some of the clubs around town were even getting robbed.

So for me, that next hustle was selling fireworks on the black market. Since fireworks were illegal in New York, the scores were always good. All we had to do was roll down to Ohio or Pennsylvania with a few trucks, load them up, and then pray that we made it safely back to New York. I'd sometimes make fifty thousand dollars in a few days.

The bills would be paid. The kids got new toys. Like they say, happy wife, happy life. But the ups didn't always last. I was still irresponsible with my money, finding ways to blow it as quickly as it came in. As a result, we never truly got ahead. Because I always wanted more. Beyond just living for the finer things in life, I was still trying to take more from it than I was giving.

Not to the same extent, but some of the same sort of people I was running around with, for all those years, were back in my life again. The life I had gotten away from for a while was still so hard to stay away from. But it didn't register as being much of a problem, since things were good again. I could handle a little chaos and craziness on the outside because I was making money. I had my wife and kids. Even if all of that, too, came at a price.

THE END OF THE RIDE

That seesaw of going from bust to being flush finally came to a halt one summer day in 2003.

It was early June, and we had made some serious cash leading up to that day. The haul for that upcoming 4th of July was good because by then we had our system down pat, and we knew all the best places to buy the fireworks. Up to that point, no one in the operation had gotten caught doing those runs for me. Those prayers of getting back to New York safely were always answered. I had the right people around me, people I could trust. It was the perfect system.

One of those people I could trust at that time was Benny. Now, Benny was an older cat—he had served in the Vietnam War and was in his 60s at the time, so he was a true red-white-and-blue American in many ways. He had put his life on the line for this country. But Benny had caught a case earlier that year. It wasn't anything to us. Small potatoes. And we knew it would be easy for him to get off. Because he was the kind of guy they'd let off easy. Guys like Benny didn't have a target on their backs, like people like me, who had long rap sheets.

But that's not how Benny saw it. He was scared to death— straight up *petrified* of doing time—which I could understand because he wasn't the kind of guy to get caught up with stuff like that. The idea of prison was so foreign to him that he wasn't able to see that they weren't looking for guys like him, they were looking for the big fish. So I kept telling him, "Benny, relax. Keep your mouth shut. You served your country. You're older. You got caught with some firecrackers. This will all blow over. Just *relax*."

But Benny couldn't relax. The thought of being locked up was too much. Around that time, he'd come to me and say, "Charl, they want me to wear a wire. They want me to do a buy and set up one of the guys. I can't do it, man."

Now, Benny was just a middle-man. He'd do firework runs for me and a few other guys. And since I was running the operation, I wasn't the one who was doing the drives, I had guys for that. A few of those guys I knew pretty well, but Benny and I were especially tight. He and I spent a lot of time together during those years. It wasn't just business, he and I were friends. We were so close that his family and mine would even go on vacation together. So, never in a million years did I think it would play out like this. Never.

Going into that summer of 2003, I told myself that this year would be different. *This* was the year we were really going to go big. I decided that I was going to buy more inventory and make more money than I ever had before, which meant the garage would be filled to the gills with fireworks, and there would be more runs than ever before. Because I wanted the big score. I wanted to take the kids and the wife to Florida, Aruba, wherever they wanted to go. Maybe buy a new boat if I had some cash left over. But no matter what, *this* was the year we were going to hit big. So I put the plans together, and that's what we did. We went big.

Benny came over around 3 p.m. on a regular summer day in New York. Kids were out riding their bikes, the mail truck was making its rounds through the neighborhood, and people were swimming in their backyards. I had been in my garage, straightening things up and filling a few orders when Benny pulled up to the house.

That was normal. During those days, he would come over sometimes three or four times a week, just to hang out. And especially during this time of year—because that was *our* time of the year, since the 4th of July was right around the corner. We were busy—business was booming. Things had become *so good* during those times that I would regularly throw parties. Huge parties for the whole block, where we'd grill out and put on a huge fireworks show for the neighborhood. If you lived on the block, chances were that you were at one of these parties. Some of them were so big that I'd spend ten or even twenty thousand dollars on a single one.

Even the cops knew what was going on, but they didn't bust our chops. I had my guys working for me at the time, and the next day, one of them would bring his landscaping truck around and we'd go and clean up the neighbors' yards. Everything got straightened up. We'd even clean the neighbors' pools, just to make sure everything was right back to where it was supposed to be. No big deal. Everybody was happy.

So Benny and I were hanging out in the yard that day, shooting the breeze, when all of a sudden, this red convertible pulled up on the street outside of my house. A red Camaro convertible, and behind the wheel was this good-looking blonde. She was wearing a tank top and her chest was sticking out. Her nails were done up all fresh and perfect like she just came from the salon. They were even painted like the American flag, all red, white, and blue, gleaming against the sun. I can still picture those nails when I close my eyes today.

The woman parked the car in front of my driveway, and then she called out, "Charlie?"

I turned to look at Benny. He looked surprised, but he didn't say anything.

I yelled back to her, "Yeah? Who's askin'?"

The woman waved me over, and when I walked up to the car, I saw that she had an order form sitting in the passenger seat. It was filled out, and she handed it to me.

"I need this filled," she said.

"And who are *you*?"

"Oh, I'm friends with the guys down at the deli," she said.

The first thought going through my head was, why didn't you give *them* the order? So I asked her that, straight up. That's when she started laying it on me, telling me how she needed the fireworks *now*. Her son was in town just for the day. She went on like that, trying to work me. It became pretty clear that she had no intention of leaving without that order being filled.

Now, that whole time, I had all the fireworks in my garage, right behind me. I knew it. *She* knew it. Everything she was asking for was there, but I wasn't buying her story just yet.

By then, Benny had walked up to the car. When I turned to look back at Benny—and I'll never forget this—he just looked at me and shrugged. "Charlie. Hook her up," he said.

Finally, I asked her, "OK, what deli? You said your friends down at the deli. What *deli*?"

Now, I don't know if this was a coincidence or what, but she said, "Johnny's Deli."

That's all it took. My *buddy* Johnny had a deli just down the street. Hook, line, and sinker, she had me. I didn't even hesitate. I went back to the garage and shut the door halfway, since I always shut the door halfway when I was doing work like that, and started to fill the order.

Benny was in the garage with me. Looking around at all the fireworks, he was surprised to see how much I had bought. "Whoa, you're really going big this year, Charlie."

"You bet," I said. "Bigger than ever before." Because this was going to be *the* year. The big score. Now, it didn't take long to fill her order because it was a small order, less than $100. Small potatoes. I was used to doing much bigger orders for people. So I bagged it up, opened the garage door, and then walked down the driveway to bring the order out to the car. The woman smiled, said thank you, and then handed me a few 20s. And then the car took off. That was that.

Benny hung around for another couple of hours before he took off. Then I went back to doing what I was doing. I just went on with my day—I didn't even think twice about what had happened.

The sun went down. Midnight, then 1 a.m. rolled around. I was just getting into bed with my wife. The kids were sound asleep. We got under the covers and settled into bed when all of a sudden there was a loud noise at the door.

BOOM BOOM BOOM.

I looked at my wife and said, "Babe, go see who it is."

Now, around that time in my life, it wasn't unusual for someone to come by the house that late at night. It wasn't totally out of the ordinary, so I didn't think too much of it. But that BOOM BOOM BOOM didn't stop. My wife got up and stood at the window to peek through the blinds. When she turned around to look at me, I saw her face drop.

She said, "*Babe*. It's the cops."

"What? The *cops?*"

"Yeah, babe. The cops. And it's not just the cops. There's like ten cars out there."

That BOOM BOOM BOOM only got louder, and it wasn't going away. Whenever it paused, I could hear my heart beating out of my chest. Finally, my wife went to open the door, and sure enough, the second person to walk into my hallway was that woman from the convertible. She had her blonde hair up, and she was wearing a uniform. In front of her, leading the way, was the District Attorney. He was all dressed up, wearing a suit and tie.

The DA said something to me like, "I take it you two know each other."

"Yes," I said.

"OK. So, now you *know* we're not messing around."

The next thing I knew, they had the cuffs on me and were tightening them around my wrists. They had their warrants out and ready. Then, behind them came a flood of people in uniforms: the DEA, ATF, and the local police. They swarmed the place in a matter of minutes. I was still in my pajamas, and my wife was out in the hall by now, freaking out. My kids were woken. But at that moment, the only thing running through my head was: this is not about my kids, or my wife. This is about *me*.

As they were dragging me out of the house in cuffs, I turned to my wife and said, "Just stay calm. Keep it together for the kids. And whatever you do, keep your mouth shut. Do not say a *word*."

Whenever they do a sting like that, the local police are present since it's in their jurisdiction. Now, they're not the ones running the show, but they're there, overseeing everything. That's why when they brought me out of the house, I was put into a regular blue and white. Right in the front seat, all cuffed up, still wearing my slippers. As I watched them turn my house upside down, a million things were running through my head.

For starters, I thought my life was over—but, I also knew that although they would likely find all sorts of stuff in the house, they wouldn't find my hidden safe. That's what kept me calm as I watched the beams from spotlights dance around my house like it was a Hollywood premier and the uniformed agents swarm the place. I at least knew that I would be able to use the money in the safe to lawyer up, and maybe the whole thing would blow over.

A few minutes later, an armored bomb truck rolled up into the driveway. By then, there were maybe fifteen vehicles in the street outside my house, and probably two dozen cops tearing through my yard. Some were in suits, others were in regular uniform. It was a real circus. I kept thinking about my kids inside the house, and how all I wanted was for the whole thing to be over.

That meant cooperating. That meant telling them where all the fireworks were, stashed in the main garage. I knew they were going to find what they were looking for, so there wasn't any use in lying or trying to cover anything up—except the safe.

It wasn't going to be that simple, though. They ransacked the entire place. From pulling out the sofa cushions to tearing apart the garage, they tore through just about everything. Of course, they found the fireworks, the stuff they were looking for. Still, that didn't bother me. That whole time, I kept praying. *Babe, keep your mouth shut. Don't say a word about the safe, and they won't know it's there. This isn't about you. This is about me. This whole thing will blow over.* Because I knew that the whole time I was in the squad car, the cops were inside the house interrogating her. They were trying to get her to crack, to tell them about the safe, or whatever else might be in the house. That's how it went in situations like this; I had seen this movie a million times.

Eventually, the DA walked up to the squad car with a detective at his side. He looked at me and said, "OK, Mr. Gilbert. So far, so good. All you have to do is give us the combination to your safe."

Fuck. It hit me like a ton of bricks: they got her to crack. Now they know about the safe, it's just a matter of time until they find out how to open it.

It wasn't until later that I found out that they played hardball with my wife. They told her that if she didn't tell them where the money was, they would bring in CPS and come get the kids, and that she would be arrested too. So, of course, she cracked.

When he said that, I knew my life was over. Like a light switch had been turned on, I became an asshole. "I have absolutely nothing to say to you until I have a lawyer present," I said to him. "And that's all I have for you."

They didn't like that. "Oh? That's how you're going to be? Alright," the detective said. "Well, I can *promise* you that we're going to blow that thing open."

I told him, "You can blow the house down. *I don't care.*"

The detective didn't like that either, and even as he was walking away, he kept jawing on about how they were going to blow the safe, no matter what.

I didn't want to think of what *that* meant for me. That whole time, I had been staring at my house in a trance. The neighbors were all outside in their pajamas and bathrobes by now, congregating as they gossiped about what was going on. Of course, they were curious: my house was lit up like a Christmas tree. On top of all the officers, they brought dogs to search the house. The bomb truck was still parked in the driveway. Even though it was the middle of the night, it didn't take long for the local news to catch wind of the whole thing. They showed up with their camera crews and lights and had a real field day with it.

Eventually, I stopped paying attention to what was happening, and for the first time, I turned to the cop who was sitting inside the car with me. He looked familiar, but I couldn't put a finger on where I knew him from. Not a minute later, a call came over the radio, and I heard his last name get called out. It clicked with me right away.

"Donnie?" I asked him.

The officer looked at me, totally stunned. "Yeah...but how do you know my name?"

At that time, I was in the program. His *father* was my sponsor. Now, I knew Donnie was a local cop, but I had never spent enough time around him for *him* to know me like that. When I told him who I was, and how I knew his father, he started to panic.

Donnie said to me, "Charlie, whatever you do. Do *not* tell them how you know me."

"Look," I told him. "I'm not an asshole. My life is in a shambles right now. But I'm not out to ruin your life. I promise, I'm not going to tell them anything about your father, or how I know you."

As we were talking, the detective came back—he was getting impatient because I still wouldn't give them any leads on the safe.

He told me that I had one more chance to come clean and tell them the combination for the safe so that we could get the whole thing over with already.

Not a chance. Again, I told the detective I had absolutely nothing to give them. Until my lawyer was there, I wasn't saying another word. That was that.

Once the detective left, Donnie turned to me. "Are you nervous about the safe?" he asked.

"Of course I'm nervous about the safe."

"What's in there?"

I didn't have to tell Donnie what was in there. All I had to say was, "Well, you know how I know your father? Just imagine."

It took him all of two seconds to put the rest together. "Fuck," he said.

After that, the conversation was over. We didn't need to say anything more about the safe, or his pops. It didn't even cross my mind to say anything about the program. I respected Donnie, and I respected his father. To this day, I still love his father. He was an important figure in my life.

The whole circus lasted a few hours. Towards the end, I saw four guys come out of my house, carrying the safe. They had blown the safe out of the wall, and now they had it. I watched the guys load it onto the truck, where I figured they were going to blow it open, just like the detective said. When I looked closer, I saw that they had taken a hose, hooked it up to my house, and ran it into the truck. Even if you don't have explosives or the combination, you can blow a safe by just using water pressure. They had a machine in the truck they could use to control the pressure of the water. It took all of twenty minutes for them to blow that sucker open.

Sitting in the squad car in silence with Donnie, I heard it before I saw anything. *Poof.* It sounded like a silenced gun being fired. Then, all of a sudden, I saw loads of water spilling out from the back of the truck. The machine got shut off, and two minutes later, it was finally over. Everything was over. They found the $25,000 in cash that I had stashed in the safe, plus the 100 grams of cocaine. And to think, they were just there for some firecrackers.

Naturally, the detective who'd wanted me to fess up and give the combination came strolling up to the squad car, proud as a peacock.

"I knew it!" he boasted. "I *knew* we were onto something so much bigger. I knew it!"

As hard as it was to keep my composure, I did. Because again, I knew my life was over. It did no good for me to banter back with him now. They had what they were looking for, and I had my ass in the car, cuffed up.

That's when I turned to Donnie and asked, "Can we just get the fuck out of here already?"

"Nah, man. We have to sit here until this whole thing is over," he said. "We can't go anywhere until they're done. After that, we'll take you down to the station and get you booked."

When we got to the station, that same detective who had been giving me a hard time over the safe was there for the booking.

"Did you change your mind about the lawyer?" he asked me. "You want to talk now?"

I had nothing to say to him. But, still, he kept trying to get my goat.

"Don't you want to know?"

"Know *what?*"

"Don't you want to know how we got you?"

"Oh, I know," I said. "I know *exactly* how you got me. That little rat friend of yours, Benny, spilled the beans. He set me up, just so he could get off the hook. Of course I know how you got me. But let me tell you something, I got lawyers. I'll be out of here before you know it. What? You think you got some big case? Pulling up with fifty boys in blue? Just watch my case. You'll see what happens."

I thought, at that time, that I knew it all. I had already been thinking of the lawyer I was going to hire for the case—this whole thing would blow over in no time. But what I wasn't expecting was what happened next.

Once they'd fingerprinted me, and we got the booking over with, and that same detective took me to the holding cell.

When we got in front of the cage, he stopped, and said, "Strip!"

So, I did. My clothes were off, and while I was standing there, butt naked, I kept being an asshole. "Oh, what? The good Lord didn't bless you?" I said to him, "I feel bad for your wife."

The detective didn't respond. All he said was, "Now, get in the cell."

I looked at him like he was crazy. "What? Get in the cell?"

"Yes. Get in the cell. Now," he ordered.

I got inside the cell and the door slammed shut behind me. Now, for anyone who's never been in jail before, I'll tell you this much: those holding cells are not just cold, they're *freezing* cold. They keep the cages that way to keep the germs out. With people coming in off the streets, they can't let anything spread.

"We'll see what you have to say in about forty-five minutes," the detective laughed. "Oh, and I'll be watching your case, alright?

You loser, you piece of garbage. We'll see what you have to say real soon."

I spent those next fourteen hours thinking of all the ways I wanted to die.

THESE ARE MY CONSEQUENCES

That whole next week, after my arrest, the news ran with my story, front and center. You would have thought they'd caught Osama bin Laden the way they plastered it all over the TV. It made prime-time news too, not just local. And because it fitted perfectly into their programming leading up to the 4th of July, they ran the story almost 24/7. That's all they talked about: Charlie Gilbert. Found guilty of illegally trafficking fireworks, in possession of one hundred grams of cocaine and a safe full of cash.

It was one thing to be dealing with that on a personal level, but it was embarrassing for my family. Fortunately, I had a good lawyer, and better still, he was part of the family. One of my cousins was a real big-shot lawyer, and he graciously took on my case. He knew me well, and he knew that I'd been messed up since my father died. He hadn't played a major part in my life up until then, but my cousin was a real figure in my brother's life. I'd always looked up to him, and I wanted to be close to him, but there was always a distance between us. It's clear to me now that he could see right through my bullshit. He knew I was living through a mask, even if I didn't.

One day, between the dates for my booking and trial, the three of us went out to breakfast—my cousin, my brother, and me. We sat down at the diner, ordered our coffee, and looked over the menus.

My cousin and I were sitting across from one another, and that's when he looked at me and said, "When are you going to learn, Charlie? What is it going to take for this to get through to you? Your wife is alone now. How is she going to hold it down with your kids?"

I stared back at him for a second. All I could say was the first thing that came to my mind: "I don't know. I really don't know. Maybe you could lend me like thirty grand?"

It took all of two seconds for my cousin to shoot me down. Given my position, and knowing his, I thought it was at least worth a shot. But I really didn't know *what* I was going to do. It was going to be hard on the kids, of course. As for my wife, I knew she was going to be fine. But I wanted her to be better than fine.

And my cousin wasn't going to let up. "Well, so what *are* you going to do?"

I sat back in my seat and gave him the most honest answer I could. "Right now," I said, "I'm trying *not* to think. I'm doing everything that I can to just not think. To stay out of my own head. I'm just trying to do the next right thing and hoping it works out."

My cousin stared at me from across the table. "What, you're just waiting for a miracle? You're no religious guy. What do you really think is going to happen?"

He had me; the only thing I could do was sit there in silence. That's when my cousin looked at me across the table and said, very seriously, "You gotta change, Charlie."

All I could think at that moment was, no, I just shouldn't have gotten caught. If I hadn't gotten caught, I wouldn't be in this mess right now. I'd be picking out a new boat, or looking at a new bracelet for my wife.

That's when he hit me with it. The thing I didn't want to hear, but needed to hear.

"All you are, Charlie, is a con man," my cousin said, with a straight face. "A fucking con man. That's it."

Hearing him say that pissed me off. As I sat there, staring at him from across the table, I thought, how dare you talk to me like that? But I was in such a state of desperation that I couldn't even argue or defend myself. In my head, he had it all wrong.

The way I saw it, my intentions were always pure—I wanted to live the way I did to create a better life for myself and my family—but really, I misunderstood my own intentions. My intentions might have been earnest, but they were never honest. I was still looking for that shortcut, a cheat code to the whole game of life, I wasn't willing or *wanting* to put in the work to build something the right way. And that's what brought me there, to that table, sitting across from someone I loved, just to hear them tell me I was a con man.

I began to think that maybe he was right. It didn't register with me right away, but what he said slowly began to resonate. It really started to sink in, for the first time ever. The days went by, and I was still all over the news—but I just kept replaying that conversation in my head. The thing was, it wasn't just me anymore, now *my family* was paying the price for my actions. Even though, to me, it was still just a few firecrackers and some cocaine.

But it *was* a big deal. And, more than anything, his words made me finally wake up and say to myself: *these are my consequences.* Because I didn't wake up every day and ask myself: who am I going to con today? In my eyes, I was no con man. *That* was the furthest thing from the truth—to me. It just happened to be that my best intentions always turned into some messed up shit.

As the denial behind my situation started to wear off, and the truth about my situation began to sink in, I started to lean on one thought: if I make it through this, and my wife doesn't leave me, I'm going to start making some changes. For real, this time. I'm not going to live up to that image of being a con man that other people saw me as. It was time to take responsibility for my actions and truly own up to my consequences.

But there were different levels to dealing with my consequences. Outside of prison time, some of that included going through the programs: anger management, how to be a good dad, all of that. The thing was, I was not a bad father. I might not have been *present*, or doing the things I needed to do to provide for my family in certain ways, but I was always trying to provide in other ways. My tendency to be irresponsible with money would usually benefit my wife and kids. I was reckless with the money I spent on them because I wanted a good life for them. Growing up the way I did, I wanted them to have more than what I had, which is what I think most parents want for their children. I just took a different path in trying to make that happen.

With each day that went by, trapped in a cell, I kept thinking about what all of this would mean for the future, for our family. *The aftermath.* The toll that it put on our marriage would be heavy, that much I knew. But, we kept it together. She stayed with me the whole time I was in there. My wife would come and visit me. There would be calls where she would tell me how she was wearing my pajamas and how badly she missed me.

As the sentence wound down, I started to have more freedom. I took those freedoms liberally, and on occasion, I found ways to sneak home. Only once in a blue moon—my time was almost up— but especially around the holidays because I wanted so badly to be with my family at that time. As anybody would in my position.

For the length of my sentence, I stuck to doing all the right things. I was working diligently, staying on my best behavior, and completing all the recommended programs to the fullest. Everything that I had to do, I was doing it. The drug tests were all coming up clean. But I was still scared of failing a drug test, even though I knew they would be clean. Because I *knew* how close I was, and I knew that Christmas was just around the corner.

Then, the day came. I walked into the courtroom with my lawyer, wearing my best suit, and I only spoke when spoken to. I remember the judge looked down at me from his stand. He set down his glasses, and said, "You should feel good, Mr. Gilbert. You worked hard for this. And it makes me feel good to say, go home and be with your family for the holidays. This case is now closed."

THE SECOND ACT

The aftermath of all that brought mixed results. It forced me to look in the mirror and tell myself the truth, that, this whole time, I wasn't doing things the right way. I was doing things *my* way, and that just wasn't working out. More than anything, I saw that by doing things my way, I wasn't being a real man about it. Any of it. Because a real man wouldn't have taken the path that I had lived for so long—lying, cheating, stealing, and doing whatever I could to make things around me *seem* good. So, I knew it was up to me to keep straight and do things the right way from there on out. That meant staying away from certain people. Because it might work for them, but it didn't work for me. I was always the one who ended up in trouble, jammed up. That was that.

The sort of trouble on the horizon, though, came in a much different form than I could ever have expected—or prepared myself for—it was the sort of trouble that would break me, again.

I was slowly building myself back up after getting out of prison. Mentally, physically, spiritually. I was establishing a better—more stable—life for myself and my family, and I was doing it with my hands. Construction, stone-cutting, all of those skills and trades that I had picked up over the years were starting to become incredibly valuable. Being who I am, I have always wanted to be the boss. Not just for the control, but because I know that I can handle it and that I do my best work when I'm the one calling the shots. I thrive under that pressure and being put in charge. So the progression to being a business owner came naturally, and it wasn't long before I had built a company that did contracting for construction work.

By that point in my life, I had become a master stonemason by trade. And importantly, over the years, I'd also built a network of people—I had my guys, and I had enough jobs to keep everyone happy and business flowing. We were crushing it on the residential level. But for as much as we were making, I always knew there was more money to be made. For myself, for my family: I wanted more.

At one point, a friend said to me, "Charlie, you should get on the bid list for some of these big jobs in the city." Little did I know that that advice would change my life as I knew it. And in ways I would have never imagined. From that first interview, when they called me in for a walk-through of the building, I crushed it. I said all the right things—because after all those years working for other people, and doing my own thing on a small scale, I was confident in myself, and what I would be able to bring to the table. It was a different ballgame, but I knew that I could hang, even if it meant breaking into a whole new bracket of wealth and responsibility. I knew that I was always cut out for that life.

I still remember that first handshake, the one that sealed the deal and landed me the bids on some of the biggest buildings in New York City at the time. They set me up with an office on Broad Street, in downtown Manhattan—we're talking serious money, but also serious potential. It all started happening quickly, that rise to the top. Before I knew it, I had dozens of guys working underneath me. And for me, going to work every day meant being in that office, overlooking Wall Street on one side and the Statue of Liberty on the other. That grind that had been on since birth was beginning to pay off in big ways.

As a kid, born and raised in New York, I spent years struggling and hustling in the streets without two nickles to rub together, so I couldn't help but stop and think, "How the fuck did I pull this off?" I wasn't the only one. Naturally, there had been people who doubted me, people who didn't think I could pull this off in the first place. But in my life, it has always been more about the people *against* me than the people rooting for me that has fueled me. And I wasn't going to let them win this time. I wasn't going to let them say, "See, I told you so."

I always knew, no matter what was going on around me at that time, deep down inside myself, that I was always cut out for a life like this. And all that time I'd spent building out a network, acquiring the skills, and making good with the right people, was finally coming together. That long road back to redemption had finally come full circle. Sure, I had never been *here* before, specifically, but I knew that this was an opportunity of a lifetime. I rose to the occasion, and with the ball in my hands now, I ran with it.

From day one, I was doing well. Real well. I'd show up at the trade meetings and crush it. Anything they asked, I did it. I became *the* guy. The proof was in the pudding: I became someone who could be trusted and depended on to do good work. And word spread quickly. At one point, FedEx was at my door every single day, dropping off new bids. At the time, it was unprecedented—I was still in my early 30s—to be an owner and operator of something this big. But I did better work than anyone else around, and that's all that mattered. My crew had a good flow too. And what really helped me continue that rise was that I wasn't the one out trying to squeeze people for every penny.

Things at home were also getting better. Each Christmas was better than the last. The wife was happy. The kids were seeing me as that supportive figure again (even if I still believe I'd always been there for them emotionally and lovingly). The respect was coming my way, in a lot of ways. It felt right. It felt deserved. We were happy. And in this life, everyone deserves the right to be happy.

My higher power was finding ways to bless me and show me the right way, which came from doing the right thing. The right thing, at that time, was to keep straight. I quit drinking and went totally straight. I knew that if I kept my head down and stayed focused only on the grind, things would work out the way they were supposed to. Doing that was a game-changer. I found myself elevating beyond just the financial side of things, but also physically and spiritually. Being straight, and seeing the results, kept me *wanting* to be good.

EMPTY PROMISES

The good times got better, even though they didn't last long. That period of my life went by fast. It was fast money, but a total grind. The cars got nicer. The house got bigger. The vacations got better, and longer. The family was happy again. And the work kept coming across my desk because word was spreading that we were the best guys for the job. People in the industry knew who to come to, and that was us. If there was a big project in the works, I was essentially guaranteed to land it; as long as I didn't drop the ball, that's just how things were working then. After a few years of doing one job, it was onto the next building. One after another, the jobs kept coming. Until they didn't.

There were a few people who saw it coming. The collapse. But not me. For me, it was like being cut down at the knees. And since I was standing taller than I ever had before, that tumble to the bottom was all the more devastating. They say the bigger you are, the harder you fall. That was true for me when 2008 rolled around and the bankroll suddenly ran out. Most of us know the story: the market crashed. People's lives were changed overnight; some were ruined. Some ended, just like that.

And just like that, the checks stopped coming in. There was always a reason—a reason to believe that it was just a snag, that the checks would be there next week. For weeks, we were promised they'd be in the mail, and everything would be good again. Some people had it worse than me. The painter, especially, got it bad. He was always the last one to finish the job—given the nature of contracting, and how the paint is always the last box to be ticked on a job—the painter got screwed the worst. You only got paid for full jobs, which meant he was spread the thinnest out of anybody. More than that, the guy was coming all the way from Poconos, Pennsylvania. To give you an idea, that's roughly a 180-mile round trip to Manhattan that he was making every single day for work. The poor guy had put so much into that job, and he was getting it the worst. It was a complete mess.

But that whole time, I was telling myself it wouldn't happen. The checks would come around. This company had been good to me. They've done me right because I've done *them* right. Just hold out—that money will be here soon. Since the company had even kicked me aces for things on projects I had done in the past, I knew I could trust them for what they said. The aces, at that time, were good. So I didn't give it a second thought, even though some of the people around me were starting to freak out—mainly, the painter.

Before I knew it, I was owed roughly $160,000 for all the work I had done up to that point. That meant the guys who worked for me weren't getting their checks. It was all starting to crumble beneath my feet, but I refused to believe it. Because frankly, I couldn't face the thought that it was. I didn't know how to confront the idea that the bottom was truly falling out.

The bottom fell out, all right. But it took us a while to feel the impact of the fall. For a while, the company was showing signs that things were on the verge of collapse. The company had brought in a new supervisor, and there were rumblings that there were problems with the general contractor.

Now, with contracting work in construction, the first six months are always the roughest. It takes people a while to get paid because it takes time to accumulate the money coming in when you're doing big jobs like that. A lot of the time, you're floating the job, waiting for that check to come. There's also a pecking order in terms of who gets paid first, so it depends on what your function is on the job, in terms of when that money does clear.

Eventually, the company we were all working for came out with the news. During one of our trade meetings, the people in charge told us that the checks weren't coming in that month—but everything was going to be doubled up the next month. We were told not to worry. The money would come. Don't quit showing up to work, just finish the job. Of course, people started freaking out. At that point, some of these people, like myself, were backlogged hundreds of thousands of dollars of pay for the jobs that had already been completed.

Even during that meeting, I was still telling myself that it wasn't going to end like that—it couldn't. That fear never really materialized for me as it did for other people. And this just couldn't happen—because I was spending it as quickly as it came in. Besides that, I hadn't actually put anything substantial into my savings account. All my eggs were in one basket, and this was it. Because the way I saw it, the company was thriving. It was one job after the next: easy come, easy go.

One month turned into two months. Still, no checks. Now people were really starting to lose their minds. But, I was still living in denial, telling myself that it was all going to get straightened out. I was so deep in it, I had no choice *but* to tell myself that. In my eyes, as long as I kept loyal and kept my head down by finishing the job, the money would come. I had a good relationship with the people running the company, and there was no reason to think that it would *not* come. I thought, at that time, they will reward me for my loyalty, for sticking through it, even though some people had dropped out—the people who knew what was coming, or at least were willing to accept it.

Slowly but surely, the evidence was starting to surface. I just couldn't get myself to man up and accept it.

THAT BLACK CLOUD

A slight breeze was blowing that day. The smell of hot dogs from the food carts came floating down the block. Taxis were flooding the streets and traffic was flowing. Newspapers were being sold at all the roadside stands. People from all walks of life were coming out of the subway tunnels, taking their coffee and briefcases to work. Anyone who didn't know what was coming would think it was just any ordinary day in New York City. The sun might have been out that day, and the skies might have been blue, but there was a black cloud hanging over me, and everyone else—we just couldn't see it yet.

When I showed up at the office, everyone was gathered around outside. It seemed a little strange, so I went to go see what was going on. I didn't even make it to the building before one of my buddies from security came up to me.

He looked at me with a straight face and said, "Charl, I'm going to give you a heads-up. You can tell anyone else you want. But, if I was you, I would go rent a truck. Right now. Pack it up with all your stuff in the office. You can always return the truck later."

"What are you *talking about*?" I asked.

"Trust me, Charlie, you're going to want that truck," he said. "Because once they lock the doors on that building, *everything* inside of it will be owned by somebody else. The banks, whoever else comes in next. They'll own everything."

I had a hard time believing him at first. But I could tell that he was serious, this was it. So, that's what I did. And I'm glad that I did what he told me to do because those doors to our building were never unlocked until the next people came in. And that was that. The market had finally collapsed. The bubble burst. The good times were behind us, at least for the foreseeable future.

Like a lot of people, I was behind on bills. There were cars in the driveway, food in the fridge, and the closets were full of clothes. But my credit was backed up to the gills. I was shaking, that whole ride back from the truck rental spot, ready to empty everything that I had into the back. It was surreal, thinking that finally, the bottom had fallen out. Those signs that I had ignored and chosen to overlook—the panic from the painter, the new supervisor taking over, the quiet, constant reminders that everything would be OK—had all surfaced, and now they were telling me: it's over.

Everything changed that day. Things got real, and I had to accept the fact that I wasn't going to be able to support my family like I had for years. There were a lot of things that we couldn't control about the situation, and even though we didn't have answers to certain questions, we knew we had each other. Another dip in the roller coaster ride of our relationship; but still, my wife still stuck by my side. She believed in me. She was a little stressed. *Who wouldn't be?* But that belief was there because she had seen me pull out of situations before. Not quite like this, but we had been there before. And we knew how to pull through.

Despite being buried in credit, I didn't have it as bad as some people. One guy even jumped off the building after hearing the news. For me, I was at least grateful that I listened to my buddy from security and emptied my office when I did because I would have never gotten any of my stuff back. Still to this day, though, I never got paid for my last jobs through the company. Not one dime. That backlog of pay—somewhere north of $150,000—never came.

Once shit hit the fan, it came down to doing what I could in the moment. That meant taking small jobs when I could get them, and slowly trying to pull us—myself—out of this hole. It was hard, though. That struggle had gotten worse than it had been in a long time. Had my wife left me during that time, I would have understood. Absolutely. All the shit that I had put her through leading up to this—and now, *this*? A lot of people would have walked away, especially after the prison stint. Most people would have reached their breaking point long before. Not her.

As supportive as they were in other ways, nobody else at that time could truly be compassionate about what was happening— because that was *always* my story.

Even the people in my family couldn't help but ask, "Charlie. We understand: this time, it wasn't your fault. But how come you didn't save for something like this? All that money you were making, and you didn't save *any* of it?" The truth was, I hadn't saved any of it—when the market collapsed, there was maybe two thousand dollars in the bank, but that was it.

Financial ruin, bankruptcy, that kind of thing can happen to anyone. People lose fortunes all the time. And this wasn't just about me—people around the world were feeling the ripple when the market tanked. But until you go bust, you don't really stop to consider what it actually means to lose it all. Losing it all was one thing, but the weight of *how it happened* was what really got me. That guilt, the gravity of the situation, was starting to weigh heavier on me than anything before.

"Charlie, haven't you noticed?" they'd say. "It's *always* something with you."

And they were right. It *was* always something with me. Why did it have to be this way? Why was I so comfortable with this feeling of being behind the eight-ball? Sure, this situation was different. But, in so many ways, it was just the same. The end result was always the same. There was always something that would bury me. From there, I began to lose self-esteem and hope.

Gradually, I slipped back into old habits. I leaned on vices, the crutches that I had kept far away from me while I was on my way to the top. Meanwhile, my wife and I kept grinding. We rode the gray area, and provided for our children the best we could. There was still food on the table and the bills were paid, but something was missing.

And, as hard as we tried to bounce back from it, we never did. Things between us started to dissolve—the weight of everything happening was becoming too heavy to bear.

Since we were always trying to catch up, but never could, our marriage paid the price. Being back at that miserable grind, it was harder to feel optimistic about what was going on around us, even if we *were* scraping by and had three beautiful children. There was no turning back from this one.

A new chapter was looming on the horizon for me, for us—but I was too naive to see it, and instead chose to deny what was going on around me. And what was going on around me, right under my nose, was that my wife was preparing her escape plan. Through the thickest of thick, and thinnest of thin, she had stuck with me. Although there were many times when she could have packed her bags, my wife was still there, she han't left my side. But finally, after all this time, she did what she should have done years before: she turned the page.

I should have seen it coming. I didn't. Looking back on our relationship, my belief today is simple: it just wasn't the time for me—she wasn't *the one*. Our purpose was to have beautiful kids, raise them, and then be happy with *someone else*.

For a while, before the divorce papers were being drawn up, we were holding it together. But things were still chaotic—we'd fight, the cops would get called—and we'd both be pointing fingers.

Things got ugly at times. But there was comfort, for me, in that chaos. No matter how messed up it was, I was comfortable living in that craziness. Like a shadow, chaos and drama had a way of following me my whole life—whether it was self-created or not—and so it became natural to seek it, even when things were going well. I'd start living normally, and then *that* became uncomfortable. Whether I was waiting for something to happen, or it was about to happen—that longing for chaos was there, somewhere buried inside of me.

But feeding my inner masochist like that was no way to truly handle a situation, even if I was not fully aware of what I was doing or how it might be affecting others. Now, as I step back and look at things, I see that sort of behavior was just a coping mechanism for what I was struggling with inside of me.

By masking, diluting, or blurring the situation with outside noise or more chaos, I could avoid answering the question: *Why am I not happy with Charlie?*

The recession, and what that meant for our family, was like a needle piercing a balloon. It didn't just deflate my ego, it drained me of all my self-esteem. To get it back, I did everything I could to try to keep things together at home. I knew that if I had my wife and kids, most of the other things didn't matter—and what I didn't have figured out, would get figured out.

So I put everything I had into being the very best husband and father that I could. For years, my wife had been the one cooking dinner for the kids, but that became something I started to do regularly. The laundry, all the little things that I overlooked before, I put my best efforts into doing. That whole time, I was telling myself that it was going to all work itself out. But it wasn't always cut and dry—the problems we'd always had were still festering.

We'd fight, and then we'd make up. But now, unlike before, I found myself begging my wife for forgiveness, for even the smallest of things. All of this only added to the lack of self-esteem, since I wasn't always standing on my two feet. But I genuinely wanted to make it work, even if that meant putting my pride aside and ignoring the signs.

The evidence was there, right in front of my face. It wasn't uncommon for my wife to ask me, "Why don't you just get an apartment?"

But all I could think was: "Why don't *you* get an apartment?"

Because I wasn't leaving my house. I knew that once I did, the doors would be locked, and nothing would ever be the same. So, it went on like that for a while, with us going back and forth. But meanwhile, that escape plan of hers was being carefully hatched— she found the best ways to get out of the marriage, the ways that would leave her most secure. Slowly but surely, she took everything from me. The house, the kids, the cars, even the damn dog.

Had I listened to the people close to me, maybe things would have been different. But the bottom finally falling out is what brought me to where I needed to be. I ended up spending a few months staying with my mother and sister on the other side of town. The wife and I were still together, but our relationship had not gotten any healthier, and it was hard to think there was a reason it was going to. That whole time, my mother and sister were voices of reason.

They were constantly in my ear, telling me, "Charl, just get out. You're the one who's suffering. Give her what she wants. You're not going to get what you want out of all of this." Maybe I could have planned better for what was to come, but all I could think to do, was to not give up. It wasn't in me to give up—and, more than anything, I wasn't willing to give up on being with my kids. But all of that created even more friction, more weight on my shoulders, more to prove. The bottom line was, I always thought that I knew something. Well, at one point, I had to realize that I didn't.

If I had listened to them earlier, maybe I would have been in a better situation when the papers came my way. Maybe I would have had more than two hefty bags full of stuff when I left my home for the last time. But I had my head in the sand, so it was hard to hear what people were trying to tell me. More than that, I couldn't see through my own ego: I was still standing in my own way. And what I started to want—once the divorce was official—more than anything, was to show *her*, and everyone else, that I could still be happy. I wanted to show them that I still deserved to be happy, no matter how much I had been through. I looked for that happiness, the fulfillment, in the most natural way I could: by chasing women again.

RETURNING TO MY ELEMENT

After spending the next few months decompressing and getting my head right while staying with my mom and sister, I left town—for good. I knew the best way to get back to being me was by getting out of the place I had spent so much time *looking for me*—that meant getting away from it all and going to New Jersey. At least in Jersey, I could be close to the beach. The beach has always been a place for me to find tranquility, and I spent plenty of days alone by the water, reflecting on life and how I wanted to make changes for myself.

Gradually, I started getting back on my bike and following my passions. Ever since I was a kid, that's what has made me tick. Building bikes, taking them apart and riding them, that's when I feel the freest. When I was doing that, no matter what else was going on in my life, nothing else mattered. They call it flow, when you're doing something you're passionate about and the world around you gets entirely tuned out. For me, reaching my state of flow meant having my hands on a bike. Being in Jersey, I was back in my element. I was working out, looking good, and feeling good.

Meanwhile, I kept busy by chasing different women. A few came and went. A few kept me interested and gave me a reason to be happy again with who and where I was. But, at the same time, I was barely making it. Being in a place like that, living right by the beach and partying regularly, I was living beyond my means. Most of what I earned went toward having fun. I never thought about tomorrow. It didn't occur to me then, but I was only chasing a fleeting moment, a good feeling. That was the cycle that I lived in, and it was what I grew comfortable with, again. The struggle. That gray area of never having enough but always having just enough to get by.

I got by alright, but the little I did have was almost always put toward that next drink, the next bag of pot, or my next meal out at a restaurant. On the surface, it might have looked fine—I had the beach life, I had friends, and I had my ways to unwind. But on paper, it was a real struggle. I was never able to catch up. Continuing to live that way was passable, but it was *not* sustainable.

At the same time, the girls were making me crazy. I also made them crazy sometimes, so I never really saw it as being as bad as it was. But still, there was always *something*. With every fight or every abrupt ending to a relationship, I was starting to notice the pattern. Even if I had broken away from that old life and the things that left me miserable back in New York, I hadn't fully broken away from the things that *kept* me unhappy and unfulfilled. That constant feeling of needing more, coupled with the cloud that I had put myself in by smoking pot regularly and casually drinking a few drinks every night was starting to weigh on me. I was living every day in a fog, but I had grown comfortable with that, and it seemed like something I could handle. I could still function.

Little by little, though, I was getting closer to the moment of clarity that I needed to reach. And then it hit me, the realization that I need more than *this*. The pattern had run its course, and this way of living just wasn't working out for me. *Something* had to change. But for something to change, *I* had to change first.

I was dating a girl in Jersey at the time this was all starting to sink in. There were points when it seemed like it could work out, and it was actually going somewhere. The bottom line, though, was we were no good together. Still, we kept finding ways to come back to each other. Only once I stepped back from that was I able to see that I needed to be honest about the situation and do something different.

The West was calling to me, and I felt that by getting out of town, for good, maybe I could find something truly fulfilling. A fresh start sounded good, but was it really the best thing for me? Before I could make a drastic change in my life, and hit the reset button—completely—I felt like I needed another perspective. Naturally, my brother was the first person I called, even though I'd been stewing on this idea of starting over for a few weeks before I finally picked up the phone.

Being the one who—I see now—always knew what was best for me, my brother was the person I looked to for advice. Even when I couldn't see two feet in front of me, he had a way of knowing what was best for me. So if I called my brother and he told me the idea was terrible, I wasn't going to do it. But, if he told me to go, then that's what I was going to do—it wouldn't even require a second thought.

My brother's immediate response when I told him my idea to pack up and drive West to start all over was to go. "Charlie, that is 100% the best thing you can do for yourself."

"Are you sure?" I asked, even though I wasn't totally sold on it.

"Absolutely," my brother said. "That's one of the best ideas you've had in a while. I think that's exactly what you need right now."

THE CHIPS ARE DOWN

So I went. The first thing to do was figure out what I had that was actually worth keeping and pack up my small SUV. In the end, I didn't take much—but it was enough. Any time you move, you realize not only how much stuff you have, but also how little you really need.

I had spent the previous month or so focused on saving up some cash to get me started and help me float for a bit—but it wasn't a large sum. I knew I would have to work hard to keep things together so that I didn't have to throw in the towel before I could even give it a fair shake.

My first stop was Tennessee. Our family had an old friend there who told me that I could stay with them as long as I wanted. Right away, I liked Tennessee. The people I met there were friendly. The sun hit a little differently, and the scenery was beautiful. There was a lot of green space and the air was clean. It was much different than I was used to, and I liked that. It felt good walking around a new town and knowing that not a single person would know who I was— you can't put a price on that feeling, and I was beginning to feel free again. But, as good as Tennessee was, I didn't feel like it was *it* for me. And if I was going to do this, and truly commit to it, by putting all my chips on the table, it needed to be exactly what I wanted. I didn't care or even know what it would take to get there—to find the *best*—but I knew that I could do it if I stuck to my gut and gave it my best shot.

Realizing what this meant, and how to make it happen, came from being able to finally shift my perspective on life. From feeling powerless at times over my circumstances—from all the previous downfalls, fractured relationships, and rough patches in my life—I was able to surrender to life a little bit. By surrendering to the things that I couldn't change, and by stopping trying to control *everything*, I started to lean on faith. Faith for what was to come. Even though I had no idea what was to come, by packing up and moving across the country with a car full of stuff, I had faith that it would work out. The way I saw it, if this was how the book was written for me, I had to accept it.

It was no coincidence that the decision to treat my mind and my body better led to fewer illnesses. I had one seizure, after my divorce, but otherwise, that was it. Finally, I was able to live without having that gnawing fear of going to sleep and never waking up. By letting go of all the stress—and the people or things that were making me miserable—and accepting my role in all of that, I was able to find my inner peace.

Forty-five years later, it was starting to finally click with me: stop clinging to the things you can't change. By channeling this new outlook on life, and eating better, I was starting to *live better*. Living better also meant removing the vices—again, I could see that without using drugs or drinking alcohol, I wasn't getting sick. That alone helped inspire me to continue that changed outlook and to live a healthier lifestyle. After all those years, I had finally taken responsibility for my health and I started to see it pay off ten-fold.

FROM CITY SLICKER TO COWBOY

After about a month of taking my time going through Tennessee and New Mexico, I decided to stop. I felt like I'd found it. *It* was Arizona, and it was October 2017. From the beautiful sunsets and open skies to the endless hiking trails and places to go mountain biking, Arizona deeply resonated with me. I felt intrinsically connected to the land. I knew right away that I wanted to stay, so I first set up shop in the southern part of the state and then spent some time checking out other towns. I began going to meetings in the area and connected with some people, many of whom remain closest to me to this day. Not only did I find my place, but I found my *people*.

More changes were going on inside my head. After so many years of being selfish, humility was starting to take hold of me. I was beginning to see how it was shaping my desires and how I chose to live. No longer was I hung up on getting the sort of job that would make me buckets of money, I was done chasing stuff; now I was chasing *me*. So all I wanted was a line of work that gave me purpose. For a while, I considered a few different types of work, but it wasn't until I went to a rodeo in Southern Arizona that I found myself thinking, man, I could be a cowboy.

Looking around at all the people in their big, shiny boots, and ten-gallon hats, and how they would smile at you when you walked by, I found myself appreciating that way of life in a way I'd never expected. It was simple, but it seemed *honest*, and it came from working hard.

The more I thought about it, the more I thought it would be pretty cool to live on a farm and be a cowboy. When I got home, I started looking into different ranches in the state and did some homework on the types of skills required for the jobs I saw posted. Having done so many jobs over the years that required physical labor and long hours, I wasn't intimidated by that side of things. Eventually, I found a job that would suit both my interests *and* my skills. A farm in northern Arizona was looking for a hand on their homestead to help with things like milking the cows and maintaining the chickens, but they also needed help building out a home on the property. It seemed like a perfect fit. I got on the phone immediately to ask about the job.

The couple who owned and operated the farm asked me to come for an interview with them, so the next day I got in my car and drove a few hours north. The more I drove, the more I realized I was going to a place where I was *really* going to be around nothing. What a difference it was going to be, from taking the train into Manhattan every day, constantly bumping elbows with people and keeping a certain appearance just to fit the part, to making my bread by putting my hands in the dirt while spending my days out in the country, working on a farm. Mind you, they weren't offering much by way of money, but it was enough.

So here I was, a city slicker on his way to becoming a cowboy. Never in a million years would I have expected my life to play out that way, and part of me couldn't help but marvel at the thought. It felt a bit surreal, thinking about how far I had come, and all that I had to go through just to get *here*. But no matter how uncertain I was as to where it was all going, I was 100% confident in what I was doing.

Intention wasn't just something I talked about, it was something that I was actually putting to form and practicing. Being more intentional with my actions was something that I was starting to take seriously, and take pride in. That commitment to my word and being intentional with my actions is what brought me halfway across the country, embarking on another new beginning, just for the prospect of something *better*. Fear of the unknown wasn't going to do me any good. And no matter what, I knew I was going to stick it out as long as I could and see where it all went because I knew that this was what I *needed*.

The owners of the farm were quick to take a liking to me. They were impressed that I'd brought my notebook with me and asked a lot of questions during the interview. Taking the job meant I would have my own corridors on the property. They were in the process of building out a main house, which became the other part of the job duty. I liked the idea of having my own space and having something that I could call and make my own again.

Part of the deal was that certain hours of each day would be spent tending to the farm. The other part of the job was to build out the main house. Since I had all my tools with me, the job sounded like a perfect fit for both of us. Anything I didn't know how to do, in terms of taking care of the animals and managing the property, I would be able to pick up. I left the farm that day feeling confident that I would be coming back to get started soon. But a few weeks went by without anything. I had applied for other jobs like it in the area, but one day, I got a text message from the couple, saying that they wanted me to start in a few days.

After packing up the car, I split from Southern Arizona and made my way north to the farm. I arrived early that morning. The couple gave me a tour of the property and showed me where I would be staying. Later that day, I drove into town, which was thirty minutes away. That's where I would have to go for any taste of civilization, since the farm was in the middle of nowhere. But I liked that; remote meant no distractions. Not having access to the internet and TV all the time ended up being the best thing for me. It helped me appreciate it when I had it, but also allowed me to not feel like I *needed* it. That same day I found my gym and then picked up a few things for the place so that I could start to make it homely and get settled.

At 5:30 the next morning, they took me through my daily tasks. The farm was set on a nice piece of land with plenty of acreage for me to explore on my off time. There were ATVs on site, which meant I could *really* get back to me and tear it up when I had a day off. But for five days a week, it was the same routine: wake up before the crack of dawn and keep busy until past dusk. They gave me a couple of hours during the middle of the day for a break, but it was basically work from sun up to sun down. I hadn't ever milked a cow before, but I got all the farm tasks down after a while. The construction side of things came easy, and in a lot of ways, I was happy to get back to working with my hands.

Even though the mornings were downright frigid—and I was having a hard time adjusting to just *how cold* the desert was at that time of year—I was good with it. Not everything about the set-up was perfect or ideal, but what I was doing was good, honest work— and that's exactly what I needed. The solitude was doing me well. It allowed me to reflect inward and meditate on some of the bigger things in life.

People mistake solitude for isolation, but there's a difference between the two. When you isolate, you do it behind a broken soul; when you seek solitude, you do so to work on the self. That solitude became something I came to genuinely cherish, and it was not taken for granted.

LIFE ON THE FARM

Gradually, I got into my flow and built a good routine. I would wake up, throw on the coffee, get my music going, pull on my boots, and then trudge out into the mud and slush under a blanket of stars; that clean, brisk air against my hands and face was a rude way to wake up. Being out there in the cold air was like stepping into a cold shower, but it kept me disciplined, and I was able to appreciate the regimen of it.

Being all alone every morning on the farm before the sun even started to come up gave me time to reflect. I had a chance to clarify not only where I was and how I'd gotten there, but more so where I wanted to be, and how I wanted to get there. As the days passed, I was beginning to realize that it was actually really quite simple. I was going to keep working hard like this, and put everything I had into being the best version of myself that I could possibly be—that meant every task would be done to the best of my ability, and each day would be treated as a new one. No longer looking into the past, or putting too much stress on the future, I was able to establish a level of presence that I had been evading for so long. And it was becoming just as clear that this might be my last shot.

It also became pretty clear, early on, that the couple who owned the farm had issues. I could smell the toxicity from a mile away. And there were some things that I couldn't help but see or hear. But

I knew that if I was going to make this last, I would have to stay in my lane and stick to the job I was hired to do. That was hard sometimes because I could see that they had their problems—and an old version of me might have stepped in and said or done something I would regret.

A few weeks into being there, they had a big fight. In the middle of the night, the husband took off and left the wife alone. When I woke up to see he was gone, my first thought was about what this meant for me. The wife assured me that everything was fine and that he would be back. She and I just had to hold it down until he *did* come back. By the way she said it, I trusted that it was true, so I kept to my business and did the job to the best of my ability.

Thanksgiving was right around the corner, and the husband still wasn't back. To celebrate the holiday, the wife took me to visit with her family, who lived in the nearest town. Right away, the family took a liking to me—even the grandkids. They could see that I was a hard worker, just happy to have honest work. Since they knew about the husband, and since he wasn't at the dinner, one of the family members pulled me aside and asked me if I could keep an eye on the wife. Of course I would, I told them. And we held it down on our own until the husband showed up about a week later.

The two of them made up, and it was right back to normal. Still, as hard as it was not to feel a certain way about it, none of this was any of my business. For me, this was about doing my time. I was there to do the work, and so that's all I focused on doing. Some days

111

were easier than others to keep my head down and lips shut because there were more than a few times that the husband would talk down to me or make rude comments. Every time, though, I let it go. In an old life, that wouldn't have been the case. I probably would have punched him in the throat, more than once. But I couldn't control how he acted, so I tried to not let it bother me.

Until one day, it got to me. I was doing a project that he had assigned me, building a chalkboard for all the daily tasks on the farm. No matter what I did, it wasn't right—he kept telling me to start the project over. Then he got nasty and started yelling at me. For whatever reason, I wasn't going to let this one slide. Not today. I had dealt with nastier people in my days, and I wasn't intimidated by him. He might talk to his wife like that, but not me. So I stood my ground. That didn't sit well with him. Nothing got physical, but we got into it.

One thing led to another, and I finally told him that I quit. I would need a few days to make my arrangements, but I was done. They would have to find someone else for the job. That was that. The husband told me that I had to leave *right then*, at that moment. I told him that was not happening. We agreed that I would finish out the week while I found my arrangements elsewhere—but I was done with the farm. It wasn't how I wanted things to end there, but I knew that I could only take so much. And, like always, I knew I would figure it out.

A few days went by before the husband approached me. "So have you made your arrangements?" he asked.

Things were in motion, and I told him that I had been working on it. "I should be leaving in a few days," I said.

Since I had planned to work on the farm for a while, I'd put a lot of work into feeling comfortable there. I had acquired a good number of things for the place to make it feel like home. That meant that no matter where I was going, I would need to make two trips out of it. I made this clear to the husband, and that's what we agreed upon.

I would still need time to map out an actual plan for where I was going to live in the long term. I liked the area and wasn't thinking of going back east any time soon. And I'd made friends there since I'd arrived. There was a buddy in Coolidge, Arizona who was going to let me stay with him while I got other arrangements in order. I had an idea of where I wanted to be, but I would need some time to iron out a few details.

The day came when it was time for me to leave the farm. Early that morning, I drove down to Coolidge with as much of my stuff crammed in the SUV as I could fit. But when I got back to the farm to make the second trip, I saw a patrol car on the property. The local police were there to greet me—and they could tell by just looking at me that I was no local. None of this helped my case when I tried to contest some of the accusations that the husband had made about me—his story was completely false, but the cops believed him over me. I *knew* that I did nothing wrong, so it was hard not to lose my cool with the cops.

Certain things were said, and then before I knew it, I was sitting in the back of their squad car. Outside, the weather had gotten nasty and there was a blizzard coming in. The whole ride down to the local jail, I was thinking to myself, here we go again. But the charges against me had no ground, so I wasn't necessarily worried about getting locked up. I was more annoyed at how everything played out. And once the cops finally did let me out, I had to wait for my buddy to make the four-hour trip up from Coolidge to come get me, in those blizzard conditions.

It was a nightmare, but we finally got out of there—and I never looked back. From there, I planned to stay with him while I got on my feet. Meanwhile, I found myself falling more and more in love with the town of Coolidge. To this day, Coolidge is a place that's near and dear to my heart. Because in a town like Coolidge, anybody who is anybody knows everybody. It had everything I needed, and I sensed in the locals an honest, hard-working mentality and a lot of humility. Being from the big city, and having been all over, I felt like *this* was where I belonged.

I decided to settle down in Coolidge, and it didn't take long for good things to start happening to me while I was there. In a short time, I found different ways to invest my money, and eventually, I turned that money into more money. Even more, I began to make strong connections there. The sudden financial upswing was nice, but I was building life-long friendships, and that's what I was so grateful for. And for all the pain and suffering my old lifestyle choices had brought me, they were starting to pave the way toward meeting more people like me and establishing myself as part of the fellowship that was formed in meeting room after meeting room. Finally, after so many years, I had found *my people*.

My people back home, especially after hearing about the incident on the farm, would call and ask me, "When are you coming home? Are you ready to come back yet?"

But the thing was, I hadn't even *thought* about going back east. I'd left that life behind in the rearview mirror, and I was bent on making it work out here. In some ways, I felt like coming out west was my last shot at getting my shit together, and if I was going to make it work, I had to keep running with the ball. Sure, things on the farm didn't end the way I wanted them to, but all I knew was that my intentions there were pure, and that each day I was doing the right thing. That meant that the small stuff was easier to get through and deal with because I could see the big picture. Finally.

At age forty-five, I'd finally found my place in the grand scheme of things, and it was starting to look a whole lot brighter. Since I was giving it my all, I was getting a lot in return. Beyond the money side of things, the relationships in my life were growing stronger. Slowly but surely, I was building out the foundations for something that I felt could be something tangible and could last through thick and thin. I was no longer only living for the moment, no longer just thinking about *me* and how to serve *me,* I was finding ways to serve my community, and to truly feel comfortable with myself. I was proud of who I was becoming, and I could see it in so many different aspects of my life. Physically, mentally, spiritually. The proof was in the pudding.

I had also begun to travel more. The meetings and groups I had found through the fellowship brought about more opportunities for travel, which is something I had not expected or imagined when I stepped into my first meeting. I had shown up there, beaten and broken, and only able to listen.

Before I knew it, I was being flown across the country to speak to a room full of a thousand people who were just like me. That sort of recognition, and the rise that I found myself back on, kept fueling my desire to do more good and to be an even better person. Much like misery loves company, this hunger for success—after seeing and tasting it—was starting to feed an insatiable desire for more success.

IF I HAD KNOWN WHAT I KNOW NOW

Success means different things for different people, but today, for me, it's feeling like I'm making an impact. Just like with this book: even if only one out of those 1,000 people in that lecture hall found something positive or inspiring from what I was saying, I was doing my job. What you take from the message and how you use it is up to you, but what I've learned, among many other things, is that everyone has a role. It's just about figuring out what yours is.

I've also come to realize I spent too much of my life in competition with everyone else. I never knew how to only focus on myself—whereas today, the only one I'm competing with is myself. If I could just be a little better, every moment, in every situation, during every experience, I win. And in a lot of ways, I feel like I have won. Because after so many years of playing the wrong games, or trying to cheat the game by making my own rules, I found the ball. Once I found it, I ran with it. And today, I'm living a life that I never thought possible. I'm proud of who I've become, and I genuinely love who I have become.

But as proud as I am, I also understand there's no room for ego in this life. Whether I'm speaking to a room full of a thousand people, or ten, it's not about *me*. Sharing this story—my story—is about finding the light in the dark.

It's when I'm in those rooms, with my people, that I get to see what has made me who I am today: for better or worse, all the things along the way that brought me high or low, have led to this. In the literal sense, I didn't even know what getting high *was* the first time I got high. My decision to get high—on the hard stuff—in the first place was made simply because I saw, in the people around me, my "friends," that I was being accepted.

So, really, it wasn't about getting high. It was about being recognized by *them* because I was doing what *they* were doing. Because I *must have* been cool if they were asking me to participate with them. Once I had that thought in my head, it was off to the races.

Anyone who knows me knows that anything I do, I do to the fullest, so it's no surprise that I took that phase in my life and went full speed ahead. At one point, I couldn't go thirty minutes without putting something in my arm or up my nose. And still, I thought that I was a functioning addict. Because I *could* hold stuff down—until I couldn't hold it down anymore. For much of my time using drugs, I made it look good on the outside until it didn't look good.

On the inside, I was still dealing with that same internal struggle that brought me to the handball courts at age 14, not knowing enough about myself to feel OK with myself, and needing to feel *cool*. Needing attention all the time, and never being comfortable in my own skin led me to a lot of places in life, and it always ended up bringing me the same results: chasing something that wasn't there.

In some ways, how I stayed down that path for so long still doesn't make sense to me. I was raised right, I just chose wrong. My parents provided for us as kids, in the important ways, even if that meant we didn't have everything that the other kids had. That was often the small things, which, to me, seemed large. When my pops would pick me up from football practice or the wrestling room, I would sometimes feel embarrassed by the car he drove—I wanted him to be driving a brand-new car, like some of the other parents, not the old beat-up cruiser that you could hear coming from down the block. I wanted new pants to start the school year, not my brother's old slacks. It's only conflicting because I know that I had their love, and I know now what love is. I know what a good relationship is—I just didn't know how to participate in those things, because of this disease that I had.

Having friends who were suffering from the same disease was a double-edged sword. It made getting high a lot easier, and something that became normalized. We enabled each other, even without always meaning to or knowing it. That made getting out of that cycle and staying clean harder. But, it's also what brought me to those rooms in the first place.

A friend of mine, Isaac, was an addict too. We had known each other since we were kids, but what I didn't know at the time was that his parents were also in recovery. He told me they'd go to these meetings, which seemed really weird to me because my parents weren't addicts. *No one* in my family was an addict. It was only me. Only, at the time, that's not how I saw it—I didn't know I had this disease.

I remember the day I brought up the idea of going to one of these meetings to Isaac. Even though I had my own company, I'd gotten high before work that day, which meant I had to be high *at work*. But the thing was, I didn't *want* to be high at work, or before—I just had no choice. Later that day, I had a breakdown at work, and something just clicked with me. When I got home, I called Isaac and asked him about the meetings. I told him I was thinking about going. Isaac thought I was messing around with him, but I was serious. He finally agreed to come with me, so we went to a meeting that was down the road at one of the churches.

His parents were there, and I remember his dad came up to me and said, "I've been trying to get my son clean forever. And watch, you're going to be the idiot who does it."

But I was scared, going into that first meeting. I didn't want anyone to figure me out. I didn't want anyone to know the truth. And then, something happened in that room. The burden of life got lighter. There was somebody there who told their story, which was really *my story*. That person and I couldn't have looked any more different if you saw the two of us standing on the street. We were the complete opposite, in every sense of the word. But that was *me*: the person who hated themselves and had a hard time looking at their image in the mirror. All they saw in the mirror was a miserable, resentful person. As I listened to them speak to the room, I broke down.

I wasn't able to lie to myself anymore. *That* was me. Sure, we had broken the cycle—my wife, my kids, the house. Now there was food on the table, cars in the driveway, and new clothes at the start of every school year. We weren't eating $1 six-packs of turkey hot dogs anymore—no more welfare cheese. We had come a long way, which is why, I thought, that the whole time I was abusing but still functioning, I had accomplished something.

But in reality, I was still dealing with the same things that I could never get over, the deep, underlying unhappiness with myself that brought me to that meeting in the first place. The realizations started to pour down on me as I thought more about my situation and how I'd gotten there. I began to see that the problems I'd had all my life started before the drugs even came into the picture. This wasn't a problem that the drugs created. But it was a problem that the drugs allowed to maintain, and ultimately feed. That problem of mine—not being comfortable or happy with *me*—was like a parasite. It was something I had been living with my whole life before the money came and went two times over. It cost me nothing to be in that room, but there I was learning one of the most valuable lessons that I would ever learn.

Looking back on it, now, I can see that that person, although they would never know it, *changed my life.* Myself, Isaac, and a handful of others—at the time, there were twelve of us—who would hang out and use together, decided to get clean. *Together*. Sadly, to this day, only three of us from that group are still alive. But we did get clean. Because we gave it our best shot. The key to that, for me, was to keep coming back to those rooms, even if it meant telling my story a thousand times over. Even if it meant having to get over the stupid—and wrong—idea that life would be boring once I got clean. When I first started getting clean, I thought life wouldn't be fun anymore. But, if that was the truth, then that's what I deserved. That was the price I had to pay; and so, I gave it my best shot.

Today, I can truly say that there is no one else I'd rather be around than my people—the ones who have suffered from the same disease and still found ways to come back to those rooms, no matter how hard it might be, or how easy it is to think there are other, more pressing things to take care of. By being in those rooms with me, they embody what it means to be humble and to have acceptance of how far they've come. It wasn't easy. And with every new story I hear, I'm reminded of not only how far I've come, but also what it means to maintain that level of normality and to be *good*.

REACHING THE UNREACHABLE

Looking back on certain moments in my life, I see not only when, but *why* I was unreachable. I was unreachable because I wasn't truly present so much of the time. But now, I do everything that I possibly can to be 100% present in everything I do. Whether that's taking the dog out on a walk, going out to dinner with my girl, or checking up on one of my people, I do my best to be *there*, at that moment. That has become so important to me as a person because I felt like there were *years* when I was not present. From physically not being present, when my wife was at home, bathing the kids, and I was at the club, dealing cards until the sun came up, to mentally not being present, when someone in my life came knocking at my door, needing me to simply *be there*.

Call it selfish, but I was incapable of being available to anyone else but myself, and that is what still bothers me to this day. Over the years, I lost a lot of sleep over it, that feeling of guilt that came from not being the friend and figure that I was supposed to be to the people around me. I'd like to think that I knew better, I just couldn't do better.

There was a particular moment in my life that stands out as an embodiment of that whole time in my life when I was simply not present. As a kid, I had a friend named James. We both had older brothers who were close in age, so between the four of us, we were tight. James and I spent a lot of time together, from kindergarten into our early adulthood. Even today, James is one of those people that I might not see for a year, but we could pick right back up and carry on a conversation as if we had just spoken yesterday. He and I remained close through a lot of changes in our own lives. Like myself, James had a grandmother that he was very close with. Our friends all knew that. We also knew that his grandmother was very sick. This was when I had just become a father—so I was roughly 20 years old—and I was at home, taking care of my newborn.

The news had made it around our group of friends that James's grandmother had passed away, late one night. That next morning, around the crack of dawn, James came to my door. I knew, up to this point, he hadn't lost anyone close to him. Whereas I had experienced a significant amount of loss already in my life, this was the first time James had to deal with something as earth-shattering as having someone he deeply loved pass away. So when James came knocking on my door, I could see that he was really upset. He told me what happened, how his grandmother had passed.

But the only thing I remember was standing in the doorway, and not really feeling *anything*. All I said was, "OK. Well, I gotta get back to the baby now." The door basically slammed in his face and then that was that. I went on with my day as if nothing happened.

I've thought about that moment so many times. I've never got over how I handled that situation, how I just could not be there for him when he needed me the most. No matter how inconvenient as it

124

might have been at that moment, I should have opened the door, invited him in for coffee, and let him get everything off his chest. He deserved that. But that thought didn't even cross my mind. All I could think about was *me*. If I apologized to James about it today, he would look at me like I'm crazy. How I handled that moment probably doesn't even come close to registering in his mind as being *wrong*.

But to me, it meant more than just not saying or doing the right thing at the right time. My actions that morning embodied how I was living. They represented how I treated the people around me, and in a lot of ways, how I treated myself. I was simply incapable of being fully present. And there are always consequences for that, whether they were something I could see or not. At the same time, I also think about those years, and how when *I* was down in the dumps or dealing with something tough, I would be wondering, why didn't anyone come for me? Why can't someone come save *me?*

It means so much to me, now, to see that, and to be able to understand how I was living because I don't live like that anymore. And I want the people I love to know that. At the same time, I do believe there's a reason I went through all of that pain and suffering, and lived with that guilt, feeling disgusted with myself at times. Even if it made a ripple in ways that I regret now, being that way was the only way I could figure out how *not to be.* And I figured that out. That's why, today, I genuinely try to put everybody else before me. Now, I'm still going to pursue the things in my life that make me happy and work for the things that I want—the nicer car, the bigger house, the better vacations—but I'm doing it differently. And by giving that back, without expecting anything in return, I feel like I truly have figured out how to live, and how to treat other people.

Because today, if someone I cared about called me and said they needed something, I would be there in an instant. I know that I could pump the brakes on whatever I was doing at that moment and take care of it—no matter what that was or what was needed to take care of it. That could mean getting a phone call in the dead of night, and then being on the next plane out of town the next morning. It could mean transferring a small sum of money to a friend who just got an unexpected bill, or is having trouble paying their rent, even if I know it might take months to get back.

Being in service to others is one of the most important things in my life now. And it will continue to be that way until the day I die. I know that my part is to be the son that I want my son to be. I need to be the brother that I want my brother to be. I need to be the friend that I need my friend to be. In all of my relationships, I have to be the love that I expect to get in return.

Humility means doing something or acting in a certain way without expecting anything in return. It's something that the world needs more of, but it's also something that can be applied to life in small ways. If you are physically capable of doing the right thing, do it—but do it in silence. If you see somebody struggling to cross the street, or needing help lifting something into their car, try to do the right thing by helping in whatever way you can, but don't expect anything in return from that person. It's easy to think that the world is messed up and will never receive the sort of help it truly deserves. But what the world needs is more humility, and that comes from looking in the mirror and asking, what can *I do* today?

LOOKING INWARD FOR ANSWERS

Doing the right thing can sometimes mean doing the hard thing.

These days, I like to buy rare, limited-release sneakers—sometimes I resell them, but more often than not I keep them for myself. Like a lot of people in the business, a passion quickly became an obsession. My girl gives me a lot of shit about having a bigger shoe closet than she does. But this particular industry can be volatile for both buyers and sellers. There are a lot of fakes out there, which means that if I do choose to resell a pair of rare shoes, I need to be 100% certain that they're real before they go back on the market.

Now, say I have a deal lined up to sell a pair of rare shoes I just bought, and I find out right before I resell them that they're fake. In this situation, the old me would have probably lashed out and done something irrational towards the person who sold them to me. That impulse in me to *react* aggressively used to dominate any reasonable thinking—immediately.

By being so quick to react and lashing out, I might fail to give that person the benefit of the doubt. Maybe they'd made a mistake, and maybe there's a better way to correct it. Suppose something like that were to happen today. I know now that the best way to handle it would be to take a step back, breathe, and figure out what *I* could do to make it right, even if it meant spending all day on the phone when I had a million other things to do, or taking a loss on the initial buy.

More than that, at the end of the day, it doesn't matter how much money I might be making, or losing, on a deal like that. If my word isn't good, nothing else matters. Even if I barely know my buyer, or we just met through an ad, I need them to trust me. Because in this life, trust is more important to me than the cars, the money, and the jewelry. You can buy all of that. You can fill your house with everything nice, but trust is one thing you cannot buy. And once it's gone, it's gone. If someone can't trust me, or vice versa, it doesn't matter what else could be made on the deal, or ones like it in the future.

I've lived that life of doing the wrong thing for the wrong reasons. Now, I feel like I found the formula for being happy, for being who I am. I don't want to go back to scratch, to ground zero—and my faith tells me that if I keep doing the right thing, for the right reason, I won't have to.

Having the ability to step back and see that, on a small level, means being the better person, even when it's difficult. That's when the big picture starts to make sense. Because the whole idea of "an eye for an eye" only leads to more suffering, and ultimately leads to more of us out there in the world trying to take more than we're giving. That line of thinking simply *does not* work.

I can personally attest to that because I have found my true peace and serenity in doing the small things the right way. So much of my life was spent carrying around this anger and resentment—it weighed on me like a wet blanket on a cold day at times—and it did nothing for me. All it did was lead to more anger and resentment. When you're walking around with anger and resentment, and you project that by doing something like giving someone the middle finger after they cut you off in traffic, or being a jerk to your neighbor because he always parks in front of your house, you're not getting anything in return. *You* are the one suffering. Because that person you're being angry and resentful towards doesn't even know that you're angry and resentful. So often, this sort of self-loathing or 'woe is me' mentality stems from insecurity, and that insecurity is something we all carry with us. How we choose to channel and empower it is what separates us from being good or bad in a given moment.

This isn't always easy to see. Some of us live with our insecurities for so long that we become comfortable with them. They're that cool pair of shades we just bought or the nice pair of slacks that we bring out on special occasions. We all have a tendency to lean on these insecurities, unknowingly, in situations when things aren't going our way or when we're in a toxic relationship. Sometimes we even shove them down and bury them until they become nothing more than an afterthought. But that afterthought can fester and become something so much bigger by not facing it head-on. By not facing the evidence, we continue to live with the consequences of our actions, which are so often, for better or worse, a byproduct of the evidence itself.

Looking inward can be difficult for us because it means applying hard, objective truth to certain things that we feel are out of our control. But by letting those things remain true in our lives, we allow *them* to take control, and that's when we start to lose control. That can be a scary thought, even if it's not always something we realize we are doing or can understand the implications of. It's easier to just allow that deeply buried insecurity or flaw within ourselves to drive our actions as we continue to fight it, all the while—most of the time—unknowingly.

For some people, dealing with things means finding reasons to be angry about everything in their life that's not going a certain way. But that approach is never going to help us get to the bottom of the issue, or whatever is causing that suffering. We all suffer. Life is filled with pain and suffering—that is the truth. No matter how much we want to avoid the fact, we will inevitably all face loss on some level. Heartbreak will happen, eventually. Fortunes are just as easily lost as they are gained. Death doesn't spare anyone. It's how we *deal* with that loss—the emotional hardship that comes from losing someone close to us, being fired from a job, getting dumped, or having an argument with a spouse—that determines how we interact with the world. And wallowing in the self-pity that's so natural and human to us is the wrong way to get through anything.

With that 'poor-me' mentality, I would still have that black cloud hanging over me. I would have never made it off the welfare cheese. I would have never been able to overcome my addictions and years of bad decisions. And I would have been locked up, a hundred times over, probably serving at least one 15 to 20-year sentence somewhere in between. I consider myself lucky to have avoided the latter, even though I came close to living that reality at certain points in my life.

But that feeling that the world owed me something didn't just start when I got caught up in the cycle of struggling, looking for a score, and being behind the eight-ball—it began at a young age. For as strong as our family nucleus was growing up, we still didn't have some of the things that other kids had. So for me, that meant taking matters into my own hands to get the things I wanted as a kid—the things that I saw other kids getting, whether that was through earning it or having it given to them by their parents.

That meant, at age 14, I was lying on my work papers just so I could get a job to pay for those new sneakers that I wanted. The ones I saw in the catalogs and commercials. Because no one was going to buy me those sneakers. No one was going to buy me a car or pay for the insurance. All of that needed to be earned, and I knew that.

But this isn't about the things I didn't have—this is about the work it took to get what I did want. Anything I wanted, especially growing up, I had to work for. And that grind didn't stop. There were days in New Jersey when I was all alone, trying to find myself, and the gas bill didn't get paid because I wasn't being smart with my money. So there were nights that I'd be sleeping in the cold, thinking I would never get through it. But, what was I going to do? Get a jar of Xanax, eat it, and just go to sleep forever? No. I was going to pull myself out of the hole. And I know now that there is something bigger than me, and it loves me, and for whatever reason, it chose me to make it through that struggle.

Our stories might be different, but anyone breathing has a 'poor me' moment. Anyone can tell a sad story of something that happened to them in their lives that made them feel bad, minuscule, or insecure. If it doesn't come soon, it will come eventually. But at the end of the day, that self-pity, that feeling that 'the world owes me' will not get us anywhere, it will only hold us back. To get through that, and truly persevere through something difficult, we have to be accountable. Accountable for our actions. Accountable for our emotions. Most of all, accountable for how we engage with the outside world, even if that means being truly present when it is painful or difficult.

THE FINAL ACT

At this point in my life, I'm not afraid of death. I'm afraid of compromising the life that I get to live. And at this point in the book, I'd like to offer you a few things to contemplate on your journey, things that I learned the long way around.

Though I'm young and healthy and have a lot of the things I've longed for and worked for my whole life, I can consider this phase of my life to be the last chapter—the final act. Because I know one thing for certain, I'm not going back. I'm not going back to my old ways of riding the gray area until it runs out, nor am I going back to being broke.

Over the years, there have been countless opportunities over the years for me to learn how to better manage my material worth. But also, how to manage myself, and how to interact on a day-to-day basis with the world. In my eyes, the realization of self is what ultimately defines our impact on the world. It's what separates us from being part of the problem versus being part of the solution.

And for as many problems as there are, there's always a solution, which is why I'm a believer that the best is always yet to come. I truly believe that. Not only because I've seen it in myself, and lived it, through thick and thin, but because I've seen it in other people. The ones who I keep close to me, especially, are living examples of what it means to persevere and make it through the truly difficult things that life can throw at you.

When you're dealing with something difficult, it's also important not to be too hard on yourself. Because feelings are not facts. It might *seem* true—that perception *is* reality—but that way of thinking can quickly lead to more pain and suffering. Clouding reality with perception is something we all do, especially when emotions are high or the situation is tense. We might try to tell ourselves that we have control over something that is completely out of our hands, but we're kidding ourselves. For example, when I was clinging to my first marriage, even though I knew that it was failing, I was suffering more than I should have because I wanted something that wasn't there. I was not willing to accept the truth. The evidence was right in front of my face, but I was too busy clouding it with emotion and fear to be able to fully accept it for what it was.

The evidence always speaks for itself. It may be difficult to realize, up close, when we're dealing with a certain problem, but it is *always* there. The evidence can be found in a good situation—like doing the right thing for someone, and the feeling it gives you afterward. But, usually when we're jammed up or trying to fix a broken relationship, we have a harder time truly accepting the evidence. We might blame a circumstance, or even someone else, when really it could be something that *we* are doing to prolong it and make it worse.

And prolonging the suffering is something that we might be doing—without even knowing or meaning to—because there can be comfort in that suffering. That cycle has a way of feeding itself, because as they say: misery loves company. That much is human, but that's where community comes into the picture. Because we can't do this alone.

A ROOM FULL OF CHARLIES

For me, the community I found after going through different programs has been by and far one of the greatest blessings in my life. Getting to know these people, even though we all come from different walks of life, I've realized that we share a similar outlook on life. We also share a similar road we've taken to get there. A lot of the people in my community, like me, doubted themselves and their higher power when things were hard. But I've learned that's the only thing that keeps you from seeing the other side.

Man would be nothing without his community. I feel fortunate to have found mine, even if, or maybe especially because, it came from living with my consequences and facing certain truths throughout my life. That same community has humbled me along the way because as soon as I enter their presence, I'm just like everyone else. It doesn't matter what kind of watch I'm wearing, or if my day was absolute shit. We're simply there to listen to one another, speak our peace, and hope that some of our struggles can help someone else get through their own.

Because in so many ways, we *are* the same, and we're not perfect. We all have our bad days, the days when we don't want to do anything but pull the blanket over our heads and disappear, or the days that we feel it's necessary to push back a little bit on the resistance that finds a way of popping up at the most inconvenient of times.

Yet, from those moments, there are opportunities to look within. Doing that means reflecting on ourselves. And self-reflection is just as important as self-love. Without understanding ourselves, we're can't fully understand other people. Without self-love, we're not capable of loving other people to the fullest, as they deserve. Since we all need love, the best thing we can do—to that person who cuts you off in traffic, or is judgmental—is to love back. *Hard.*

My whole thing is this: love hard on *everyone*. Especially the ones you can't stand. Next time that person you can't stand is being a jerk to you, love *extra* hard on them. Show them what it means to be nice. See what happens when you do. That alone can be hard. But by breaking down those walls they're living behind, you can make an impact on someone. That's when we start impacting the world.

Living this way takes practice. Trying to positively change someone's day means taking your own ego and setting it aside for a minute. Now, it might not click with that person who is being a jerk to you right away, but if they see that you are being genuinely nice to them, consistently, eventually they'll be able to see how *they* are interacting with the world. Just because they might be choosing to punish the world with how they project themselves, that doesn't mean that you have to do that too.

Because who am I, who are we, to punish someone else when we don't even know what it's like to walk a day in their shoes? We don't know their definition of pain. We don't know how much they've suffered up to that point. Maybe that person who's being a jerk is having a day that's so bad you can't even imagine what they've been through. They could be on the brink of a total mental breakdown, and your reaction could be what sends them over the edge or brings them back to earth. Doing something positive, something as simple as sharing a smile with them, or passing along a compliment, could be all it takes to totally turn their day around. For the people in our own circles, this could mean reaching out with a phone call, even if you know *exactly* how that phone call is going to go. The small things might seem insignificant on the surface, but that sort of behavior and goodwill can become contagious.

By doing that sort of thing, you might not know it, but you could be doing more than turning someone's day around. You might be saving someone's life. By making that one phone call to lift their spirits or help them get out of a quick jam, you might just be that deciding factor that makes them think all is not lost. So no matter what is going on in our own lives, we should never feel too busy or bothered to do the small things for people, especially the ones we love.

Living this way has allowed me to find inner freedom in life. And anyone can find this freedom. The freedom to be you, to move on, to be happy. Because if you do it long enough, and everyone starts to know what you are all about, they'll see you coming down the street and know *exactly* what sort of energy you're going to bring. It truly does have an effect. Hopefully, they can also start to put that goodwill into practice and begin to be better towards themselves, and ultimately to others.

And it goes both ways. That negative person, the one who's a jerk to everyone and constantly pushing back on life, can bring down a room just as easily. Being the emotional creatures that we are, we pick up and carry the energy of the people around us. That miserable person only pushes people away. People can *see* what they're all about. And ultimately, being that way leads to a life that lacks the love and deep connection with the people around us that makes life worth living.

CONFRONTING OUR FLAWS

Insecurity drives all of us. In so many ways, we allow it to determine how other people see us. And with that, our flaws can become magnified into something much bigger than us. We allow them to stand in our way without even realizing it, which is why, so often, the less we have, the more we try to take. Trying to take more than you give will never get you the results you want. I'm a perfect example of this. I've walked in those shoes a thousand miles over. And all I've found is the same inner void. The inner void that only craves more emptiness and self-pity. That misery which loves company.

But for as real as that misery feels, you'll find it becomes powerless when you stand up to it. That's when you discover another truth: that feelings are not facts, and you have power over them, just like you do over your circumstances.

The power we have over our circumstances might appear minuscule, or at times non-existent, especially when shit gets heavy. But make no mistake about it, *we always have power within our circumstances.* Certain circumstances in life might require us to surrender more power than others, but once we determine what our *own power* is within that circumstance, that's when we can manage it to our fullest ability. No matter what, we have to take accountability for what our role is within that struggle we might be facing. Because, without taking responsibility for actions or emotions, we'll only continue to fall into a cycle of self-loathing, inaction, or low self-esteem.

At times, when my self-esteem was at its lowest, I felt like I had no power. I felt like my life was over. There was no good way to spin it. I convinced myself that I was going to die in the shoes that I had been walking in, without any money in my pocket, once I had found a bridge to sleep under. The hope that I had for life became so bleak that all I could see were black skies.

But no matter how bad things were, I took it upon myself to control whatever it was that I could, even if that meant the little things. When the little things became big, and when I was back on top, I told myself that it would never end. The cash would always keep flowing. My view, from up top, would never be obstructed. This was *mine*, and it was made for me. And the foundation of that thing I had spent years building would never crumble. Of course, it couldn't.

When it did crumble, though, the only person I had left to answer to was myself. So often, I was the one standing in my own way, but I was too proud or stubborn to admit it. By removing my ego from the picture, that's when I started to have clarity. I began to see not only what I had been living without, but also what I had been blessed with this whole time. Love, unwavering support from the people in my life, and an unrelenting work ethic. Knowing that has led me to live with so much gratitude. Had I been able to tap into

142

those things like I do now, and find ways to give back, but also be good to myself, I'm convinced that I would have been a multimillionaire ten times over.

But that's not what this is about. This is not about what *could have been*. This is not even about where I am now, which I consider to be a good, and financially stable place in life. For me, it's about the decisions that I made to get here. Even if those decisions meant doing things the long way, through honest, hard work. Had things fallen apart right away on the farm in Arizona, I told myself that I would have been just as content shoveling mud, or being a door-greeter at Walmart, just to pay my bills and put some food on the table. Because after having it all, and losing it a few times over, I found that it wasn't about the money at all. It was about doing something to the best of my ability, and not worrying about what it meant for my wallet or how people saw me.

When I started to do that, things truly started to pan out for me. And the money came too.

Money, for anyone, can help certain problems go away or give us comfort in how we go to bed at night, knowing that the bills will be paid and the lights will stay on. Money can buy us the finer things in life—and as much as I enjoy the luxurious things in life, they're not what drives me. What drives me is the opportunity to use that money to do something good. That could mean buying up a few hundred dollars worth of toys or candy on a random day during the summer and dropping it all off at a local hospital for the nurses to hand out on their own time. That could mean donating to a certain organization that I believe in. It could mean buying a sandwich for the guy on the street corner instead of handing over a few bills. Those decisions can seem small—like a drop of water in the ocean—but they can also have a big impact on the world—a butterfly effect. Because every wave that has reached shore started as something minuscule—a mere drop of water—before it made the impact of shaping something bigger than it. The laws of momentum are real, and good actions have a ripple effect.

FAITH & GRATITUDE

Being where I am now means that I have different problems to worry about. But as much as I dread the tax man, I never would have imagined that I would be in a position to have to worry about the amount of money I made in a single year. For that, I am truly grateful. Turning what seems to be a problem into a blessing is one of the best things we can do for ourselves. The glass is half full. Because without gratitude, there is little that we can truly hold on to in this world. So many things in life are fleeting, but finding the gratitude within ourselves, and applying it to a certain situation, is how we can truly fill our lives with more.

More than once, you'll come across the word GOD in this book. That's not what this book is about. The word God has different meanings to different people, and I think that's beautiful. But for me, living a Godly life has put me in this position to be "successful" and to be able to sit down and write this book in the first place. Because I went through a lot of life suffering from the thought that, if there was a God, he hates me—he's busy with all the good people on this planet and doesn't have time for me and my suffering. But the people that I have been fortunate to spend most of my time around, mostly through the program and fellowship, were able to bring me to a better perspective: he wasn't neglecting me—God was there the whole time, he was just waiting for me to get my shit together. Once I started to realize that, I was able to see how blessed

I was, to have made it this far in life, because at times, I never thought I'd get past that next struggle.

Again, God can be whatever you choose it to be, but everyone needs something bigger to believe in. Whatever we perceive that higher power to be, it's important to find it.

Attaching faith to that higher power is also how I began to live a better life. Because faith is right there with gratitude—both are necessary for getting through the good or the bad moments in life. When things are spiraling around you, and nothing seems to be working out, or you've just lost that job you worked so hard for, how else are you going to get through it, without faith that something better is waiting around the corner?

Maybe you're presently going through a hard moment. But if you're sitting there right now, reading this book, know this: you *got through* those moments. Because, again, I've had so many of those hard moments, times I thought I'd never get through it, but what kept me going was my faith that I would. Practicing that faith, constantly, has put me in a position to see that it does pay off. And seeing it pay off has only led me to want more of it, and to live that way, every single day. Seeing it pay off, and understanding how it has allowed me to give back and pay it forward, is what truly touches my soul. Like misery and how it loves company, this sort of feeling is contagious, and I've come to see firsthand how it can create more good for the people around me than any paper envelope filled with money.

THE VIEW FROM THE TOP

Money, to a certain extent, has brought me here, but I continue to chase it because it has allowed me to stay here. Here, is Hawaii: my paradise. I knew from the first time I saw those white sands meet the crystal clear waves of the ocean from the oval window of the airplane as we descended on the main island, that *this* was my paradise. I had a lot of work to do to make that paradise my home, for good, but there was no doubt in my mind that I had finally reached the place that I had been looking for and working towards my whole life.

Hawaii has so many beautiful places and an abundance of beautiful people, but to me, it signals something greater: I made it. I might have squandered opportunities along the way—a hundred times over—to accumulate the sort of means that it takes to have *made it* here, but the fact is: I made it.

Might I have been more comfortable had I connected the dots ten years ago? Without a doubt. But there's something inside of me that stood the test of time: my work ethic. My grind has been on since birth, and it's a gift. That hustler mentality was only being applied in the wrong ways. I was no good at being a criminal, but I came to realize that I could apply those skills of hustling—that inner perseverance—toward something much greater. While the good things have come my way over these last few years, and I have built a comfortable life—one that I am never content with, though—the greater good has become about providing for not only my family and the friends I have accumulated across the world, but also for my own fellow man.

Because I know that in many ways, that person I see on the street without shoes, or holding a sign as they ask for spare change, is no different from me. Not only who I used to be, but also who I am today. And for that reason, I constantly look for ways to inspire and impact people. That may come from telling my story, or taking a moment to ask a stranger how their day is going, but that desire is to do good—because when I do the right thing, the right thing comes back to me, one-hundred-fold. That idea remains so deeply entrenched in me that I know it won't fade or burn out.

ACKNOWLEDGEMENTS & A TASTE OF WHAT IS TO COME

Like the struggles, without the people in my life, I wouldn't be here. There are too many people to thank for keeping the faith in me and picking me up when I needed it the most. Countless times, certain people could have given up on me. They could have thrown in the towel on me entirely and told themselves that they'd be better off now, without having to deal with my bullshit. But what brought me through so many dark moments was their unrelenting love and support.

Of those people, I would like to thank my brother David, my sister-in-law Diana, my sister Meredith, my three children, Taylor, Michael, and Bayley, and my precious little granddaughter, Giuliana. I'd also like to thank my late mother, father, and grandmother.

And of course, she probably thinks she's being left out, but I have to include a big thank you to my girl, Becky, because without her I wouldn't be here, and none of this would be possible. I'm a believer that behind every man is a good woman, and she's every bit of that. Everything about her makes me want to be a better person, and the person that I try to be today. Your support, Becky, is what allowed me to see what I was missing in myself, and also in life. I'm grateful for the hard times we had, just as much as I am for the good times. Without you, I wouldn't be able to share my message with people, which I hope becomes a source of inspiration and hope.

Just as I am grateful for all the good faith that came from people in my life, I'm thankful for the doubters. The people who doubted and rooted against me, for different reasons, are also the ones that built me into the man that I am. Because I can honestly say that wanting to prove those people wrong fueled me as much as my desire to make proud the people who never left my side. And I'm proud of the struggle, I wouldn't change a single thing about the path that brought me here. Truly, not one single thing. Because it's a constant reminder of what we do, why we do it, and what the results can be.

But if there is one thing I'd wish for, it's one more **TUNA CASSEROLE**. One more Sunday night around the dinner table with the people I love. Because once that tuna casserole hit the table, nothing else mattered. There was no thinking about money problems, or how we'd make the next mortgage. All of our problems melted away, and we could just enjoy each other's company.

So if you enjoy what you've read, stay tuned. Because I think I can smell a **TUNA CASSEROLE** coming out of the oven right now.

ABOUT THE AUTHOR

From New York, Charlie Gilbert grew up in a working-class family but fell into the wrong crowd early on. Living a life of cheating, stealing, and hustling in the streets, that search for the next big score or shortcut led to dead ends and suffering. After numerous broken bones, dozens of stitches, and years of battling addiction, Charlie turned his life around and became a contributing member of society—the honest way. But when what's now known as the Great Recession devastated the global economy, Charlie lost nearly everything. Needing someone to believe in him and give him another chance, Charlie found that person. It was him all along. His story of redemption and recovery is a testament to the perseverance and grit that a man can pull from his gut when the odds are stacked against him and the chips are down. As a successful entrepreneur, Charlie's story illustrates what can happen when we start believing in ourselves and doing the right thing, even when it's hard, inconvenient, or seemingly small.

www.ingramcontent.com/pod-product-compliance
Lightning Source LLC
Chambersburg PA
CBHW060531130626
46553CB00002B/714